Loth
Berwicks

C000240605

Keith Fergus

60 walks

*A comprehensive guide to walking on
Scotland's south-east coast, including
a seven-day trail from
Berwick-upon-Tweed to Queensferry*

Contents

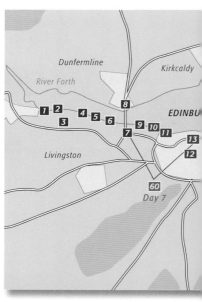

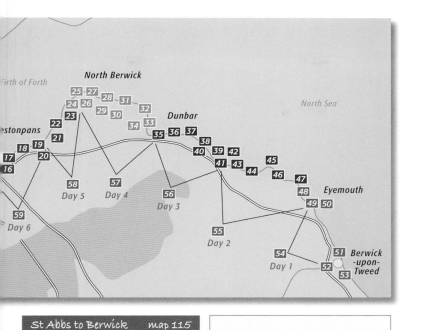

Title page: Coldingham Sands at sunrise

Published by Mica Publishing
Text and photographs
© **Keith Fergus 2014**

ISBN **978-0-9560367-5-9**

Title page: Coldingham Sands at sunrise

Maps & design: **Mica Publishing**
www.micapublishing.com

Printed and bound in India by Replika
Press Pvt Ltd

Mica walkers' guides are distributed
by **Cordee Ltd**; info@cordee.co.uk,
www.cordee.co.uk

While every effort has been made to
ensure the accuracy of this guidebook,
paths and access points change over
time. Sturdy footwear and waterproofs
are recommended for all walks, plus a
map and compass for all upland walks.

Lothian & Berwickshire Coast

Path above Linkim Shore

cotland's eastern seaboard is seen, by many, as a poor relation when compared to its west coast cousin. Yet its history, wildlife and scenery are easily on a par with the more renowned western fringes and its geology is possibly the most significant in the country.

This is certainly true of the Lothian and Berwickshire coast, which stretches for approximately 161km (100 miles) from the Forth Estuary just west of Edinburgh, to the historic and welcoming town of Berwick-upon-Tweed. A coastline which passes through four regions and two countries and offers some exceptional walking.

The early stages along the Firth of Forth, from the City of Edinburgh into East Lothian, are punctuated with soft, sandy beaches and low-lying dunes. But as the coastline turns south from Dunbar, through the Scottish Borders, and into Northumberland and England, it becomes increasingly rugged, with an almost never-ending barrier of cliffs rising to a height of more than 152m (500 feet).

Even with this diversity of landscape the variety of walks will surprise many. Beach, woodland, riverbank, lochs, countryside, cliffs and urban walking can all be enjoyed when following the 60 routes within this guidebook.

An excellent road and public transport infrastructure means gaining the start point for the majority of routes in this guide is relatively simple and with attractive towns and villages scattered along the coast, such as Bo'ness, Queensferry, Aberlady, North Berwick, Dunbar, Cockburnspath and Eyemouth (as well as Edinburgh, Scotland's capital city), a selection of pubs, restaurants, shops and

accommodation is never far away.

60 walks are described within this guidebook. 53 are between 3km (2 miles) and 14.5km (9 miles) in length and are perfect for a morning or evening stroll or an invigorating half-day ramble. The final seven combine to make a superb 145km (90 mile) coastal trail, which can be completed in one long memorable walk, or split into seven enjoyable day hikes. Whichever route is chosen, it will not take long to recognise that this is coastal walking at its very finest.

History

The coastline of the Lothians and Berwickshire offers a clear window into the age of the earth; whether this be the remains of volcanic activity or tangible proof of rocks dating back an incomprehensible amount of time.

The geology is at its most striking as you travel along the Berwickshire coast, particularly between Barns Ness and the village of St Abbs. Here beds of sedimentary rock, including sandstone, mudstone and coal, were formed during the early Carboniferous period, some 360 million years ago, when the seas were tropical in their temperature, giving rise to great coral reefs – try dipping your toe in the North Sea today and you will see things have changed markedly over the subsequent years.

The coastline also yields clear evidence of the earth's movement over this massive timescale, with great deposits of layered rock running along the fine cliffs between Siccar Point and Berwick-upon-Tweed. The renowned geologist James Hutton confirmed his theories regarding the age of the earth when visiting Siccar

Barns Ness Lighthouse

Point in 1788. Several very important fish fossils, thought to be over 400 million years old, have also been found at Newhaven, on the outskirts of Edinburgh.

Volcanic activity is apparent when climbing the likes of North Berwick Law and Arthur's Seat, which rises above Edinburgh's city centre. Both were formed around 350-300 million years ago and today grant the finest views along the coastline.

Humans have been exploiting the coastline for several thousand years, particularly along the more sheltered south bank of the Firth of Forth. Discarded hazelnut shells have been found on Cramond Island and carbon dated to 8,500BC when Mesolithic hunter-gatherers fished the waters of the estuary and hunted in the surrounding woodland. In 2002, excavations in Dunbar revealed a house from this period.

The estuary and coastline aided transport for our earliest ancestors and small communities built up along the coast and on the low-lying hills over the course of the next few thousand years.

However, like much of Southern Scotland, it was the Romans who really established themselves, particularly along the Firth of Forth. Roman Forts were established near Musselburgh, at the mouth of the River Esk, at Cramond (which translates as Fort of the Almond), and, perhaps most famously, near Bo'ness where the trans-Scotland Antonine Wall terminated in AD142.

Over the subsequent centuries, after the Roman occupation had ended, several major settlements developed at the likes of Berwick-upon-Tweed, Dunbar, North Berwick and Musselburgh. Many towns were built around harbour's including ones at Leith, Aberlady, Port Seton, Cove and Eyemouth, with fishing becoming the dominant industry. Saltpanning, shipbuilding, coal mining, mills and agriculture have also played a key role in the development of communities over the past few thousand years.

John Muir with a pint of Fowlers; Prestonpans Mural Trail

John Muir, born in Dunbar in 1838.
Sent forth an idea which inspired the nation of America and indeed the world for generations to come.

The least we can do is stand him a pint of Fowlers.

R Elliot

Aberlady Bay

Lothian & Berwickshire Coast

Newhaven harour

Today many of these industries have gone or play a far less significant role in the economy. Now the more contemporary industry of 'the outdoors' is a focal point for an ever-burgeoning tourism and recreation sector with the likes of golf, cycling, sailing, wildlife-watching and, of course, walking, playing an increasingly important role in local economies.

What to See

The coastline between Bo'ness and Berwick-upon-Tweed is filled with a magnificent array of sights and sounds. There are several historic and fascinating buildings visited during many of the walks within this guide, ranging from contemporary architecture such as the Scottish Parliament in Edinburgh to ruins like St Helen's Church, near Siccar Point, which dates from the 12th century.

Other intriguing structures include Kinneil, Newhailes, Dalmeny and Gosford Houses, the castles of

Blackness, Tantallon, Dunbar and Fast, lighthouses at Fidra, Barns Ness and St Abb's Head, and the historic and much fought over walls of Berwick-upon-Tweed.

But perhaps the most celebrated examples of the stunning architecture to be found along the coast can be seen spanning the Firth of Forth and linking Queensferry and North Queensferry.

The Forth Road Bridge and, particularly, the Forth Rail Bridge have gained mythical status due to the amazing construction process that took place during the 19th and 20th centuries and they remain iconic symbols of Scottish heavy industry and civil engineering.

Throughout the 60 walks the scenery is never less than compelling. The views along the early stages of the coast extend north to the Ochil Hills and beyond to the big mountains of the Southern Highlands, including Ben More, Stob Binnien, Stùc a' Chroin and Ben Vorlich, while a good portion of Southern Scotland can be observed from Arthur's Seat.

Across the Firth of Forth the Fife coast, with the twin dimples of East and West Lomond always prominent, is a constant companion until the East Lothian coastline heads south into Berwickshire. From here the high cliffs afford a wonderful prospect to the rolling Lammermuir Hills and on into Northumberland.

But it is the wildlife that can be spotted throughout the year that really raises the this coastline onto another level. Wherever you walk, the diversity of flora and fauna is remarkable.

This may be at specific sites such as John Muir Country Park and St Abb's Head or when simply strolling along a beach or riverbank; whooper swans, wild geese, little egret, whimbrel, greenshank, oystercatcher, sandpiper, dunlin, knot, curlew, ringed and golden plover, kittiwake, skylark, meadow pipit, shags, fulmars, herring gulls, puffins, frogs, toads, butterflies, damselflies, wood anemone, wood sorrel, red clover, red campion, sea pinks and common spotted orchid is just a selection of what can be seen.

The beach, cliff, woodland, riverbank and urban settings all add something to this magnificent coastline and make walking here an absolute joy.

Lothian Coast from Arthur's Seat

Using this Guidebook

Route Maps & Mapping

Route maps accompanying the walks are drawn from out-of-copyright one inch Ordnance Survey (OS) mapping and half inch Bartholomew mapping, supplemented by in-the-field GPS tracks, and personal observation.

These route maps are only sketch maps and walkers are advised to purchase the up-to-date Ordnance Survey Landranger (1:50,000) or Explorer (1:25,000) scale maps for the walks.

The relevant OS Landranger map for each walk is indicated by 'OS 65' etc in the information panel
<www.ordnancesurvey.co.uk>

Map Symbols
P Car park or layby
P Other parking
▲ Summit
⛳ Golf course

Route Symbols
—— Route on path
······· Route no path
=== Road
━━━ Route along road
===== Track
▪▪▪▪▪ Route along track
- - - - Other path
—— Optional extension

• routes on roads generally follow pavements or verges.
• tracks include all non-tarmac surfaces (farm and forest tracks), and All Terrain Vehicle (ATV) tracks on open hillsides.
• 'pathless' hillsides are often criss-crossed by paths created by sheep, deer, cattle or goats.

Access

The Land Reform (Scotland) Act 2003 grants everyone the right to be on most land and inland water for recreation, providing they act responsibly. These rights and responsibilities are explained in the Scottish Access Code <www.outdooraccess-scotland.com>

• take personal responsibility for your own actions and act safely;
• respect people's privacy and peace of mind;
• help land managers and others to work safely and effectively;
• care for your environment and take your litter home;
• keep your dog under proper control;
• take extra care if you're organising an event or running a business.

Grades & Times

Most of the routes in this guide follow maintained paths suitable for a variety of abilities. A few, however, take rougher or upland terrain where paths are less obvious. The following grades have been used.

• **Easy**: Low level waymarked routes on mostly level terrain.
• **Easy / Moderate**: Low level waymarked routes, but longer or with inclines or rougher terrain.
• **Moderate**: Higher level routes over hills or moorland, on generally well-marked footpaths.
• **Moderate / Strenuous**: Low and high level routes over some rough terrain. There may be little waymarking and paths may be indistinct in places.

Grading walks is very subjective. For this reason, distance and terrain should

also be taken into account when choosing a walk.

Timings are for round trips and include stops for lunch, rest and admiring the view. However, these timings also have a subjective element and the time you take on your walk will be influenced by factors such as fitness, terrain, the nature of the party (large groups are generally slower than small ones) and the weather.

Equipment & Weather

During the spring and summer months the Lothian and Berwickshire coast is, on average, sunnier with less rainfall than its west coast cousin. During autumn and winter the North Sea winds can be strong and bitingly cold and this should be taken into account when walking longer distances during these seasons.

Many of the walks are along exposed cliff-tops and particular care should be taken when walking children and dogs. High winds can also be an issue, as can the tide on some of the routes. It is recommended that walkers check the state of the tide before commencing these routes (see below).

The weather can vary significantly from place to place and from hour to hour, so waterproofs and warm clothing are recommended. Stout footwear with a good tread is advisable for all walks. Adequate food and water should also be taken, although many of the towns and villages along the coast have Visitor Centres, shops and cafes.

Weather forecasting is not easy, but the following websites are worthwhile.
<www.metcheck.com>
<www.bbc.co.uk/weather>
<www.bbc.co.uk/weather/coast_and_sea/tide_tables>

BBC tv forecasts can be accessed via terrestrial and satellite services.

Travel

General: Traveline Scotland (0871 2002233)
<www.travelinescotland.com>
Bus: Eves Coaches (01368 865500)
<www.evecoaches.co.uk>
First Group (01324 602200) <www.first-group.com>
Lothian Buses (0131 555 6363)
<www.lothianbuses.com>
Perryman's Buses (01289 308719)
<www.perrymansbuses.co.uk>
Prentice Westwood (01506 871231)
<www.prenticewestwoodcoaches.com>
Rail: Scotrail (0845 6015929)
<www.scotrail.co.uk>

Bo'ness to Cramond

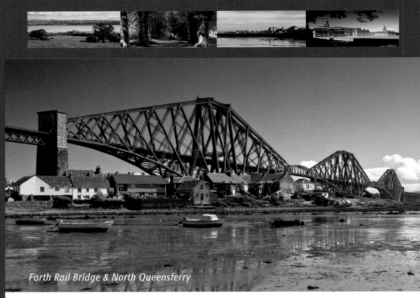

Forth Rail Bridge & North Queensferry

he Firth of Forth is a constant companion throughout the walks detailed in the first three chapters of this guidebook. The nine walks in Chapter 1 follow the early stages of this magnificent estuary, bookended by the fine, historic towns of Bo'ness and Queensferry.

In-between, notable and significant buildings such as Kinneil House, House of the Binns, Blackness Castle and Hopetoun House provide interesting focal points to several of the walks, as do the celebrated Forth Bridges at Queensferry. Whatever the location there is a wonderful assortment of wildlife, fascinating history, sumptuous scenery and a warm welcome around every corner.

The town of Borrowstouness (better known to many as Bo'ness) is home to two different walks, one of which makes its way around **Kinneil Estate** [1], (site of a Roman Fortlet at the eastern extremity of the Antonine Wall) and another through the **Bo'ness Nature Reserve** [2], where a glorious array of wildlife vies for attention, along with the great views.

Heading east and another estate, **House of the Binns** [3], offers a hill-top vantage point over the Forth, whilst **Blackness to Abercorn** [4] is linked by a dense slice of broadleaf woodland with historic Blackness Castle at one end and the 12th century Abercorn Church at the other.

Part of **Hopetoun House** [5] was

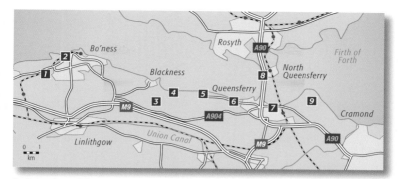

built by the celebrated architect William Adam, and many see this magnificent structure as his finest work. Make up your own mind by following the paths and tracks around the estate, where impressive woodland and striking views surround the house – internally it is equally impressive and well worth the admission fee.

The estate grounds are also the starting point for a simple but thoroughly enjoyable walk from **Hopetoun to Queensferry** [6].

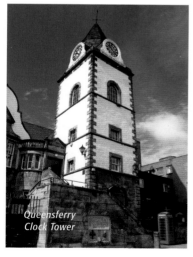

Queensferry Clock Tower

Peaceful paths and country roads lead into the lively town of Queensferry, where there is an extensive array of independent shops, cafes, bars, restaurants and accommodation. A quiet road then returns to Hopetoun House along a scenic section of the Firth of Forth.

Historic Queensferry [7] is flanked by some lovely woodland and an attractive elevated walk around the southern edge of the town utilises paths and tracks lined with wildflowers and offers some fine views across the estuary to the Fife Coast.

Dominating the town are the two **Bridges Across the Forth** [8]. The Forth Railway Bridge and the Forth Road Bridge (soon to be joined by a third crossing) are both incredible feats of engineering that span the Firth between Lothian and Fife. A walkway over the Forth Road Bridge offers a spectacular vantage point up and down the river and is easily followed to North Queensferry from where a train can be taken back over the Forth Rail Bridge to Queensferry.

The final walk in this chapter is a circular route round **Dalmeny Estate** [9], encompassing established broadleaf woodland, a 13th century tower house and 17th century mansion, and a good portion of the attractive Lothian coastline.

Kinneil Estate
James Watt & the Antonine Wall

Old Kinneil Church

A walk around Kinneil Estate packs much history into its short distance. The excellent Kinneil Museum provides a good starting point, both for the walk and to learn more of the estate's history and that of the Romans who constructed the Antonine Wall here in AD142.

From the 14th century Kinneil Village grew around Kinneil Church and by 1661, 559 people lived in Kinneil parish, most within the village. However by 1667 it was cleared, due to major redevelopment of Kinneil House, with most of the villagers moving to Bo'ness. Robert I had granted the lands of Kinneil to the Hamilton family in 1323 and between the 15th and 17th centuries Kinneil House took the form of a separate tower house and palace.

Much of the house's extension, between 1667 and 1688, was under-taken by William and Anne Douglas-Hamilton (the Duke and Duchess of Hamilton) and saw two decorative towers connecting the tower house and palace culminating in the imposing stately home we see today.

Unfortunately the house is not open to the public but the parkland is open daily and the museum Monday to Saturday from 12.30 to 4.00 pm.

From the museum follow a red gravel path towards Kinneil House then turn left to its far left corner, go through an opening in the wall and turn right. Ahead lies a little ruined building, dating from 1769, once a workshop used by James Watt, the great Scottish inventor and engineer.

Cross a bridge, high above a deep gorge and burn from where the path turns right and continues to reach the remains of Kinneil Church and village, where only the church's western gable

START & FINISH: *Kinneil House car park (NT985808)*

DISTANCE: *3.5km; 2 miles*

TIME: *1hr*

MAP: *OS 65*

TERRAIN: *Tracks & paths*

GRADE: *Easy*

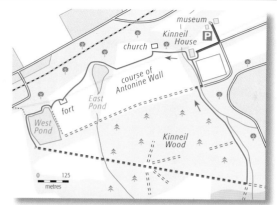

Bo'ness on the Forth.

Once past the fortlet the path climbs a flight of wooden steps to a fork. Go right, walk through pine woodland to the right of West Pond. Take a path on the left and walk anti-clockwise around the pond.

At the south-western edge of the pond turn left at a fork onto a broad track, which enters woodland. At a cross-roads go straight on where the track climbs gradually eventually arriving at another crossroads. Turn left onto a woodland path, which descends gradually down to a junction, where there are fine views of the Southern Highlands. Turn right, walk through a car park and over a bridge crossing a burn then bear left onto another path and walk back to Kinneil House. Go through the gap in the wall, and return to the car park.

and some gravestones are still visible.

Turn left from the church then right onto a grassy path, which continues through the parkland of Kinneil Estate. The path soon enters a pocket of woodland from where it swings sharp right and travels anti-clockwise around the East Pond. It then continues to the left of woodland passing the impressive remains of a Roman fortlet, part of the Antonine Wall, the line of which passes through the estate to its conclusion at

Kinneil Estate

2 Bo'ness Nature Reserve
Industrial heritage on the banks of the Forth

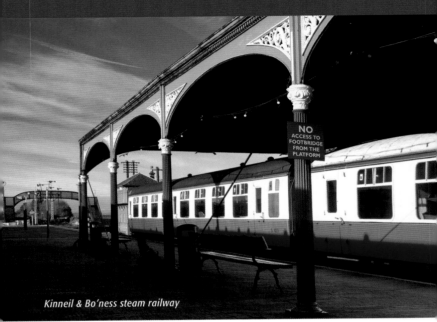

Kinneil & Bo'ness steam railway

The history of Bo'ness (or to give the town its full name Borrowstouness, the Burgh Town on the Ness) dates back to AD80 and the Roman invasion by Agricola. In time, Bo'ness marked the eastern extremity of the Antonine Wall, linking a series of forts from the Clyde to the Forth, see **Kinneil Estate** [1].

Industries such as salt panning, fishing (Bo'ness had a recognised port from the 16th century) and, in particular, coal mining were all vital in the further development of Bo'ness; the 12th century monks at Holyrood Abbey were given the coal works at Carriden Estate, the earliest reference to coal mining in Scotland and in 1291 the monks of Dunfermline Abbey were also given rights to dig coal from outcrops around Bo'ness.

By the 19th century Bo'ness had two pits employing around 700 people, the last of which closed in 1983. The town is also home to the Bo'ness and Kinneil Railway and museum and 8km (5 miles) of track operated by the Scottish Railway Preservation Society. Kinneil Nature Reserve was built on the site of an old colliery. It is extremely popular with walkers and birdwatchers and home to alder, willow, Scots pine and birch, with resident and visiting birdlife including knot, dunlin, oystercatcher, grebe, duck, teal and avocet.

From Bo'ness & Kinneil Railway

START & FINISH: Bo'ness &
Kinneil station car park (NT003818)

MAP: OS 66

DISTANCE: 5km; 3 miles

TERRAIN: Roads, tracks & paths

TIME: 1hr 15mins

GRADE: Easy

Station, walk past the station, turn right over the fine railway footbridge, and drop down to Bo'ness Harbour. Turn left and follow a path in-between the railway line and harbour. At a cross-roads go straight on, following a surfaced path along the foreshore and enjoying stunning views of the Ochils and Southern Highlands. The path hugs the coastline, passing through a strip of woodland to an information board as the nature reserve is approached.

Winding wheel

Turn right here and follow a grassy path to the left of a tidal island. As you pass this the path peters out for a short distance but is soon picked up again where it continues west and then south through the peaceful reserve – there are superb views across the Firth of Forth to Grangemouth Refinery.

At the southern edge of the reserve bear left at a fork onto a surfaced path, leading through more woodland. At the next fork go right then straight on at a crossroads (signposted Kinneil Halt) from where the path drops down by a level crossing and then climbs to a

junction.

Turn right then immediately left at a fork back onto the outward-bound path. Retrace your steps towards Bo'ness but upon reaching the fore-shore turn right at a fork, carefully cross a level crossing, walk through a small car park and turn left onto Kinneil Road (A904).

At a roundabout bear left onto Memorial Drive and follow this by the Winding Wheel, a fine memorial to mining and the miners of Bo'ness. Continue onto Union Street, pass the Post Office (the building dates from 1911) and the 18th century Customs House back to the railway station.

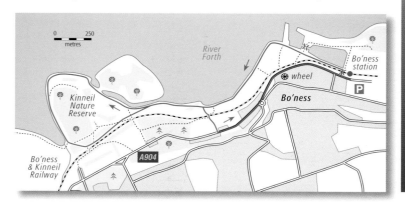

House of the Binns
Hilltop home of the Dalyells

Binns Tower

he House of the Binns has been in the care of the National Trust for Scotland since 1944, but its history stretches back to the early 17th century when it became the seat of the Dalyell family.

Edinburgh merchant Thomas Dalyell purchased the estate in 1612 and between 1621-30 he completely redesigned the original house. Little remains of Dalyell's work having been extended during the 18th century, taking on the more baronial appearance we see today whilst internally the house was also intricately decorated.

Perhaps the houses' most famous resident was Tam Dalyell (1615-85) who was a General during the Wars of the Three Kingdoms and, due to his skirmishes with the Covenanters, became known as Bluidy (Bloody) Tam. Dalyell formed the legendary Royal Scots Greys here in 1681.

The estate is open daily, closing at dusk whilst the house opens between 1st of June and 30th September, Saturday-Wednesday 2-5pm. Where livestock graze in fields please keep dogs on leads. From the car park go through a gate into the grounds of House of the Binns. Immediately bear left then right and follow a grassy path, enjoying fine views of the Ochil Hills. Continue through a pocket of woodland and climb a flight of steps to reach a track, signposted for Binns Tower. Go straight on and exit the woodland by a gate. A short, steep slope ascends to gain the impressive Binns Tower, which

START & FINISH: House of the Binns car park (NT 051786)

DISTANCE: 3.5km; 2 miles

TIME: 1hr 15mins

MAP: OS 65

TERRAIN: Roads, tracks, paths & fields

GRADE: Easy/Moderate

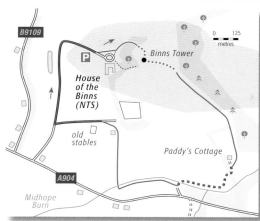

Binns Tower

House of the Binns (NTS)

old stables

Paddy's Cottage

Midhope Burn

B9109

P

A904

0   125
metres

direction, to reach a track.

Turn right, then left past Paddy's Cottage (once home of a farmhand called Paddy Gallacher) onto a rough single-track road, which veers right to skirt more woodland. The road crosses the Errick Burn then bears right, just before the A904, to pass through a gate. Following the course of the burn, a fenced path strikes through attractive countryside to a wooden footbridge. Turn right, cross the bridge and go through a gate into a field. Make your way north across the field culminating at a gate near a cottage.

was built in 1826 by Sir James Dalyell apparently because of an after-dinner wager. The tower sits atop a grassy knoll and grants a spectacular vista that includes the Pentlands Hills and Blackness Castle.

From the tower walk east across a field, passing a trig point and a large oak tree, to reach a strip of woodland. Turn right and walk along the field edge, keeping the wood to the left, descending gently to a gate. Go through it, bear right and walk diagonally across a field, in a south-westerly

Beyond the gate, bear left onto a track and walk through another gate, just left of an old walled garden. Turn left, follow an estate road by the cottage and an old stable block, once home Royal Scots Greys horses. Continue back to the main estate road, turn right, and follow the road as it climbs gently back to the car park.

Old stable block

Blackness to Abercorn
Tracks & paths through Wester Shore Wood

Abercorn Church

*H*istoric Blackness Castle is the starting point for this fine walk, which also visits Abercorn Church. Blackness Castle's turbulent history dates back to the 15th century when it was built by the Crichton's, at the time one of Scotland's most powerful families. King James V then converted it into a key artillery stronghold, in no small part due to its position on the edge of the Firth of Forth.

Blackness Castle survived many attacks until Oliver Cromwell's vast army forced a surrender in 1650, attacking the castle from both land and sea. Blackness Castle was also used as a state prison and ammunition depot and today is under the care of Historic Scotland. Open daily between 1st of April and 31st October and every Saturday-Wednesday between 1st November and 31st March and there is an admission charge.

From Blackness walk along the shore road, past Blackness Boating Club, and just before the entrance gates to Blackness Castle, turn right through a gate, climb a flight of steps, follow a path alongside the castle walls and down more steps towards the Forth.

A path then veers right onto an area of grassland, which makes its way south above a beach, with superb views of the Forth Bridges. The path swings right alongside the Black Burn then turns left over a bridge and passes through a gate into Wester Shore Wood.

A fantastic track (Cycle Way 76) runs parallel with the shore and makes for easy, pleasant walking. Woodpecker, great tit, and redstart enjoy the tree canopy and scatterings of bluebells and wood anemone grow on the woodland floor during spring and summer. After approximately 2.5km bear left at a fork and drop down over Nethermill Bridge, which crosses the fast flowing Midhope

START & FINISH: *Car parking near Blackness Castle (NT 054801)*

DISTANCE: *8km; 5 miles*

TIME: *2hr 15mins*

MAP: *OS 65*

TERRAIN: *Tracks & paths*

GRADE: *Easy/Moderate*

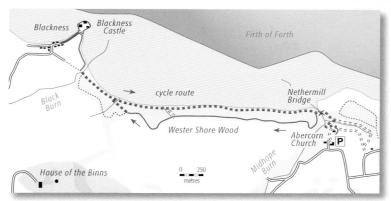

Burn. The track then swings right to reach a signpost for Abercorn Church.

Go right, cross a bridge over the Cornie Burn then follow a good track as it zigzags up an embankment. At the top of the climb turn left, follow a track a few metres and pass through a gate into the grounds of Abercorn Church.

A section of this stunning little church dates from the 1100s having been built on the site of a 7th century monastery. Most of the building, along with many of the gravestones, date from the 17th century and the kirkyard includes the burial chambers of the Dalyell's of **House of the Binns** [3] and the Marquises of Linlithgow. Internally Abercorn Church is equally charming, and much of it intricately decorated.

Retrace steps over Nethermill Bridge but then take the left fork onto a rougher track, which climbs steeply, veering right to another fork. Go right, back into Wester Shore Wood and follow a good path along its southern perimeter, high above the coastline. As the trees thin there are some fine countryside views. The path undulates easily through the woodland, eventually dropping back down to the shore track. Turn left and retrace the outward route back to Blackness.

Blackness Castle

Hopetoun House
West Lothian's 'Little Versailles'

Hopetoun House

*H*opetoun House is one of Scotland's finest stately homes and the paths that encircle the house and estate present a really fine walk, with open views across the Firth of Forth and lots of wildlife.

Sir William Bruce designed the original Hopetoun House in 1699, having been commissioned by Charles Hope, who would later become the 1st Earl of Hopetoun – see **Hopetoun to Queensferry [6]**. It was completed in 1707 but in 1721 the renowned Scottish architect William Adam was asked to enlarge the house and his design, which was inspired by the Palace of Versailles in France, was added to the front of Bruce's building. Hopetoun House is generally accepted to be Adam's finest work. Internally Georgian and Edwardian design play host to an extensive array of artworks and furniture.

Within the gardens stands a yew tree (thought to be 550 years old), a 300-year-old Cedar of Lebanon and a giant North American redwood alongside cypress, beech and oak as well as a colourful mixture of wild and garden flowers. Hopetoun House and grounds are open daily from the end of March to the end of September. There is an admission charge to the grounds and house.

From the ticket office exit right onto the main estate drive and follow it away from the house through lovely parkland. Once through a gate bear right onto Cycleway 76 and follow the narrow estate road to a fork. Go right, follow the road to a junction and keep straight on through a gate where a track continues to the left of a wall at the edge of the open grassland of the deer park.

Walk past the remains of Staneyhill Tower, which stands to the left, and at a cottage turn right, cross a cattle grid and follow the estate road back to the ticket office. Make a left onto a pedes-

START & FINISH: *Hopetoun House car park (NT090789)*

DISTANCE: *4km; 2.5 miles*

TIME: *1hr 20mins*

MAP: *OS 66*

TERRAIN: *Tracks & paths*

GRADE: *Easy*

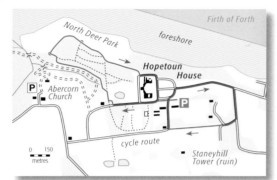

Firth of Forth

North Deer Park

foreshore

Hopetoun House

P Abercorn Church

P

cycle route

Staneyhill Tower (ruin)

0 150
metres

treecreeper and coal tit may be spotted. In due course the track sweeps right to run above the coast from where there are amazing views west to Blackness Castle – see **Blackness to Abercorn** [4] – the Ochil Hills, Ben Lomond and Ben More.

This gorgeous section of the walk continues east above the North Deer Park (home to the Hopetoun Red Deer) via the West and East Bastions of Abercorn Castle, a one time Clan Douglas stronghold captured and destroyed by James II in 1455. The bastions offer fine views east to the Forth Bridges and Queensferry.

Continue on to Hopetoun House and once through a gate swing right around the front of the house back to Lime Walk, turn left and return to the car park.

trian walkway called the Lime Walk, a beautiful tree-lined avenue. Follow this past Hopetoun House and just before a gate bear right onto a woodland path then right onto a track to reach a pond and the classic view of Hopetoun House. What you see here is Sir William Bruce's design.

Continue past the pond then take the left branch of a fork, where a track proceeds through woodland to the right of a wall – chiffchaff, goldcrest,

Forth bridges from Hopetoun House

Front gates – Hopetoun House

Woodland paths and quiet country roads link Hopetoun House with Queensferry and both locations are ideal to wile away the hours. From Queensferry it is a pleasant walk, predominantly along a quiet section of the Lothian coastline back to Hopetoun House, ancestral home of the Hope family for over 300 years.

The family's origins date back to the early 1500s and their wealth greatly increased in the 17th century when Sir James Hope married the Leadhills mines heiress Anne Foulis. It was their son, John Hope, who purchased the lands surrounding Abercorn in the late 1600s with the intention of building a fine mansion house. Unfortunately John Hope drowned in 1682 on board the shipwrecked Gloucester and it was his son Charles who eventually commissioned the building of

Hopetoun House in 1699 – see **Hopetoun House [5]** for more info. The house and its grounds are open daily from the end of March to the end of September and there is an admission charge.

From the ticket office exit right onto the main estate drive and follow it away from the house through lovely parkland. Once through a gate bear right onto Cycleway 76 and follow the narrow estate road to a fork where the cycleway goes right. Continue straight through woodland, bearing left at the next fork.

Walk along the estate road, in due course passing two stone gateposts beside a cottage. Keep straight on through scenic countryside past another cottage from where a path goes through a gate then keeps right at a fork. Upon reaching a wire fence the path runs to its left and past a factory.

START & FINISH: *Hopetoun House car park (NT090789)*
DISTANCE: 9.5km; 6 miles
TIME: 3hr 15mins

MAP: *OS 66*
TERRAIN: *Roads, tracks & paths*
GRADE: *Easy/Moderate*

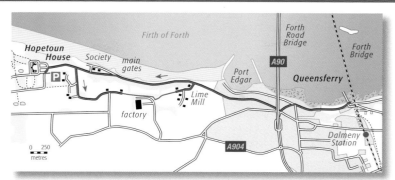

When the fence veers right continue straight on then bear left onto a paved path, which descends through a gate.

At Lime Mill, make a left, descend to Society Road and turn right. Cross a bridge and follow the roadside verge past Port Edgar as it climbs towards Queensferry. A pavement is soon picked up. Walk past King George V Park onto Hopetoun Road, which soon veers left underneath the Forth Road Bridge. Hopetoun Road then drops down into Queensferry. Go left onto High Street where the hospitality of Queensferry, and fine views, can be enjoyed.

From Queensferry retrace your steps to Lime Mill but keep straight on along the quiet Society Road, which continues west along the coast, where a variety of wading birds, swans and mallards can be spotted. The pleasant mixed woodland of East Shore Wood runs to the left of the road and there are lovely views along the Firth of Forth towards the Ochils Hills. About halfway along the road an opening in the low sea wall gives access to the beach which, depending on the state of the tide, can be followed to another gap before the road forks to the houses at Society.

Keep left at the fork and go through the impressive entrance gates, back into the grounds of Hopetoun Estate. Follow the magnificent drive as it climbs gently through gorgeous woodland. Keep straight on through a gate and continue back to Hopetoun House.

Hopetoun Estate

Historic Queensferry
The pilgrim's ferry to Fife

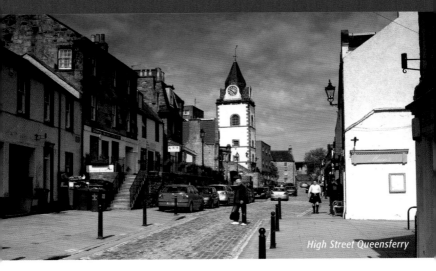

High Street Queensferry

*I*t was in the 11th century that Queen Margaret (wife of Malcolm Canmore, King of Scotland) established a church at Dunfermline and paid for a ferry service to transport pilgrims, on their way to St Andrews, across the Forth Estuary. Subsequently the village of Queensferry grew along the narrowest point of the channel (a little over a mile separates Queensferry from North Queensferry on the Fife coast).

The monks of Dunfermline Abbey initially operated the ferry service and a variety of ferries ran for several centuries until the road bridge opened in 1964; see **Bridges Across the Forth [8]**. During the 1950s the Queensferry service was the busiest in Scotland with four ferries annually carrying 1.5 million people, 600,000 cars and 200,000 goods vehicles by 40,000 ferry journeys.

Queensferry's narrow but attractive High Street is lined with several inter-esting buildings, including the Tolbooth (adorned by a striking clock tower), which dates from 1887, and the Ferry Tap pub, the building dating from 1683. The oldest building in Queensferry is St Mary's Episcopal Church, which was built in 1441.

Facing the Forth Rail Bridge at Hawes Pier, beside the Lifeboat Station, turn left and walk along the promenade, beside New Halls Road, onto the cobble-stoned High Street. Turn left onto The Loan, where the pavement climbs quite steeply, passing Hawthorn Bank and Stoneycroft Road on the left. Just before Queensferry Parish Church turn left onto a lane signposted Back Braes/Ferry Glen.

Follow the lane along Back Braes, which travels high above the town and past a viewpoint, providing a fantastic

START & FINISH: *Car park at Hawes Pier (NT137784)*
DISTANCE: *4.5km; 2.75 miles*
TIME: *1hr 25mins*

MAP: *OS 65*
TERRAIN: *Roads, tracks & paths*
GRADE: *Easy*

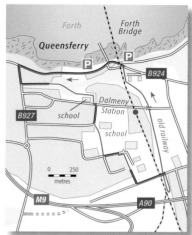

Once past Queensferry High School make a left into the grounds of Queensferry Recreation Centre beside a cycleway sign for Edinburgh/Dalmeny.

Follow the cycle track past playing fields to a junction, turn left, then continue through woodland onto Scotstoun Avenue. Cross the road, turn left and follow the cycle track as it swings right by some houses and drops down to gain another junction. Turn left, walk along the cycle track through more woodland towards the village of Dalmeny. Beyond a gate, cross a bridge over a railway line, turn right and descend to a cycle/walkway beside the railway line.

Walk right, follow the track back towards Queensferry passing Dalmeny Station, and eventually underneath an archway of the Forth Rail Bridge. Once under a footbridge, but before a stone bridge, turn right and follow a path alongside a fence. It swings right to a steep flight of steps on the left. Descend these and return to Hawes Brae (B924) at Queensferry. Turn left and walk back to the start.

view of the world-renowned 1890 rail bridge and the road bridge. Descend a flight of steps then turn right into the tranquil woodland of Ferry Glen. The path is easily followed over a foot-bridge and up more steps. At the next junction, turn right over a footbridge to gain Station Road. Turn left then immediately right onto Ashburnum Road.

Forth Road Bridge from Back Braes

Bridges Across the Forth
Iconic engineering for rail, road & foot

*T*wo of Scotland's most distinctive structures begin (or end) at Queensferry, crossing the Firth of Forth to end (or begin) at North Queensferry. This fantastic walk exploits both with the Forth Road Bridge walkway granting a scenically spectacular walk. The return journey crosses the Forth Railway Bridge by train from North Queensferry.

The railway bridge is one of the finest examples of engineering in the world and the statistics of its construction are astonishing: opening in 1890 it took 4,000 men seven years to build at a cost for £3.2 million. Construction involved over 54,000 tons of steel and 6.5 million rivets yielding a length of over 8,000 feet. When the Forth Road Bridge was opened in 1964 it was the longest suspension bridge in Europe

utilising 39,000 tons of steel. The opening of the bridge effectively ended the ferry service that had crossed the Forth for centuries.

From Dalmeny Station, cross Station Road onto a wooded path signposted Hawes Pier. Follow the path then descend a flight of steps beneath the Forth Railway Bridge. Turn left onto a narrow road then immediately right onto a path, which swings right to another flight of steps on the left. Descend to Hawes Brae (B924), turn left, follow New Halls Road past Hawes Pier onto High Street. Walk through Queensferry bearing right onto Hopetoun Road and continue out of the town.

Once across Stewart Terrace, turn left onto the Forth Road Bridge cycle/walkway and climb underneath the great platforms of the bridge onto

START & FINISH: *Dalmeny Railway Station car park (NT138779)*
DISTANCE: *5.5km; 3.5 miles (train)*
TIME: *1hr 45mins*

MAP: *OS 65*
TERRAIN: *Road, tracks & paths*
GRADE: *Easy*

Sunrise on the Forth Rail Bridge, North Queensferry

centre of North Queensferry, which is an attractive and quiet little village, dominated by the road and rail bridges, and one that owes much of its existence to quarrying and the ferry service that ran for centuries across the Forth to **Historic Queensferry [7]**.

At The Brae, turn left and climb the steep slope passing Jubilee Well, an ancient spring, which was used for centuries to relieve tired and thirsty travellers. At the top of The Brae, bear right underneath the railway bridge onto Brock Street then left to North Queensferry Railway Station. Either take the train back to Dalmeny and Queensferry or return on foot via the road bridge (**11km, 7 miles, 3hrs 30mins**).

its east side. Turn right and begin the spectacular walk across the bridge. The walkway runs beside a cycle track and is separated from the road by a barrier – keep to the walkway as maintenance vehicles sometimes use the cycle lane. A gentle climb, then descent into Fife offers sumptuous views of the Fife and Lothian coastlines, the Forth Railway Bridge, and the Pentlands Hills.

Once off the bridge turn right and descend steps to gain the B981. Carefully cross the road, (it is a tight bend) and turn left then right through a gate signposted North Queensferry. Descend more steps then walk along a tarmac path onto Ferry Barns Court. Turn left then left again onto Ferry Road, which climbs gently back to the B981.

Bear right and descend into the

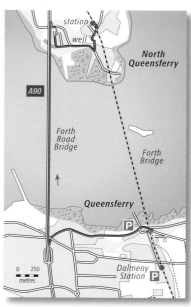

Dalmeny Estate
Woodland tracks & sea views

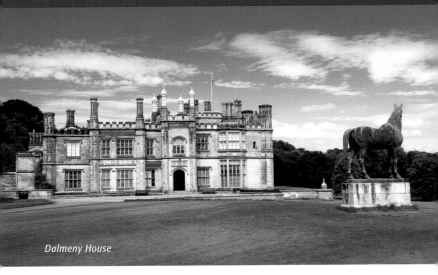

Dalmeny House

A little to the east of Queensferry is the wooded parkland of Dalmeny Estate. The grounds, which include the attractive Dalmeny House – see **Cramond & Dalmeny [10]** – and the curiously named Barnbougle Castle have been owned by the Earls of Rosebery since 1662.

Barnbougle Castle is a tower house, its history dating back to the 13th century. During the 17th century it became the Rosebery family seat and is now a grade-A listed building. Its unusual name may translate from Gaelic as Point of the Marsh. An assortment of paths and tracks meander through the grounds, linking easily, via the village of Dalmeny, with Queensferry.

From Dalmeny Station, cross Station Road onto a wooded path signposted Hawes Pier and follow this to a flight of steps which descend beneath the Forth Railway Bridge. Turn left onto a narrow road then immediately right onto a path, which swings right to another flight of steps on the left, which lead down to Hawes Brae (B924).

Turn left then right onto a single-track road just before the Forth Rail Bridge. Follow the road as it hugs the coastline, soon passing through a gate into Dalmeny Estates. Continue past Long Craig Pier then some houses onto a lovely estate path (also Cycleway 76), which progresses through woodland. Follow the path as it makes its way past Peatdraught Bay and around Hound's Point to continue south-east by the secluded Fishery Cottage.

Keep on along the path to a junction. Go straight on where an estate road

START & FINISH: *Dalmeny Railway Station car park (NT138779)*
DISTANCE: *8km; 5 miles*
TIME: *2hrs 30mins*

MAP: *OS 65*
TERRAIN: *Road, tracks & paths*
GRADE: *Easy*

travels along a gorgeous stretch of coastline, home to some charming secluded beaches. Walk past Barnbougle Castle and through gorgeous broadleaved woodland. In due course the road exits the woodland at Drum Sands, where there are lovely views across the Firth of Forth to the Fife towns of Dalgety Bay and Aberdour. The road then climbs gradually, bearing right to the magnificent Dalmeny House.

At a crossroads go straight on and walk along the estate drive as it meanders through open countryside (keeping dogs on leads) for another 1.5km, culminating at the B924. Leave Dalmeny Estate by carefully crossing the B924 onto a minor road, which is followed for just under 1km into the charming village of Dalmeny, which

grew as a planned village in the early 1800s to serve Dalmeny House. Dalmeny is also home to St Cuthbert's Church, thought to have been built around 1160.

Walk through the village along Main Street then go straight on across Standingstane Road, onto a narrower road. Just before a railway bridge turn left onto a cycle/walkway, signposted Dalmeny Station and Queensferry. Descend the path and then turn right, pass under a road bridge and follow a wildflower-lined path for approximately 500m towards Dalmeny Station.

Just before another road bridge, bear right up a flight of steps onto Station Road. Turn left, cross the bridge and walk along Station Road, passing underneath a railway bridge to return to Dalmeny Station.

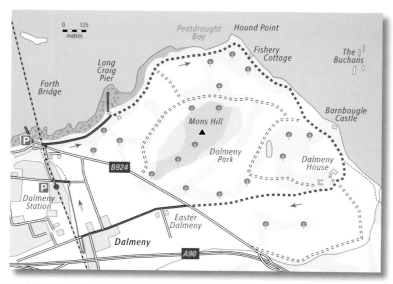

Cramond to Gullane

Poppies near the site of the Battle of Pinkie

Continuing from the historic village of Cramond the Lothian coastline skirts the fringes of Edinburgh and its suburb's including Leith, Portobello and Joppa, to reach East Lothian at Musselburgh. On the outskirts of Musselburgh is Fisherrow and here the John Muir Way begins – or ends – its 72km (45 mile) journey to Dunglass.

The John Muir Way hugs the East Lothian Coastline throughout this chapter and forms the basis for many of the walks in and around attractive places like Prestonpans, Cockenzie & Port Seton, Longniddry and Aberlady. A couple of the walks also venture inland into Edinburgh to sample the delights of Scotland's capital city.

The River Almond Walkway at Cramond provides a marvellous start point for exploring **Cramond & Dalmeny** [10] and east along the fore-shore to **Silverknowes** [11], with the novel option of crossing a stone causeway to Cramond Island – but only at low tide!

Heading inland and the volcanic land-scape of **Arthur's Seat** [12] sits slap bang in the middle of Edinburgh. It is a steep climb onto the summit but the panorama across Edinburgh and along the coast is breathtaking. Staying in Edinburgh, the city's extensive cycle paths present a gentle, scenic stroll to visit **Leith & the Botanics** [13].

The charming and bustling environs of **Portobello & Joppa** [14] are lovely

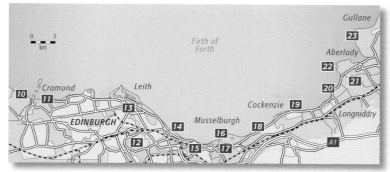

to wander around. Portobello has a magnificent stretch of sand and a variety of pubs and cafes granting a relaxing environment in which to spend a few hours. Nearby is **Newhailes House [15]** a fine Georgian mansion maintained by the National Trust for Scotland, where paths and tracks circumnavigate the estate and surrounding countryside.

Lothian then becomes East Lothian at Musselburgh, which is one of Scotland's oldest and most attractive towns. The John Muir Way is followed from **Fisherrow to Prestongrange [16]** via the nature reserve of Levenhall Links with its magnificent array of wildlife and some exceptional views. Housed in the former colliery, Prestongrange Museum describes the days when Coal was King, and is well worth a visit.

Musselburgh & the Esk [17], which cuts the town in two, is another beautiful walk. It visits the site of the 1547 Battle of Pinkie, a clash that claimed the lives of around 6,000 Scots soldiers. Prestonpans is home to the **Prestonpans Mural Trail [18]**, an unusual but fascinating walk that visits a number of beautiful and thought provoking murals within the town, detailing its absorbing heritage and culture.

The coal-fired Cockenzie Power Station then dominates the coastline as the walking continues east into the villages of Cockenzie and Port Seton. Beachfront promenade and woodland paths connect **Cockenzie & Longniddry [19]** with the return journey along the beach and dunes of Longniddry Bents.

Exceptional scenery and wildlife are a feature of the out and back route along the John Muir Way from **Longniddry to Aberlady [20]**, which passes to the north of **Gosford Estate [21]** on the outskirts of Aberlady. The grand 18th century Gosford House lies at the centre of the estate, surrounded by woodland paths and informal gardens. These two walks are easily combined, or can be enjoyed separately.

The chapter's final two walks cover the coastline to the east and west of Aberlady village on the edge of Aberlady Bay. Scenic paths traverse **Craigielaw Point [22]** offering striking views west to Arthur's Seat and the Edinburgh skyline and the long, rolling ridge of the Pentland Hills.

Aberlady Bay was designated Britain's first local nature reserve in 1952. This stunning slice of East Lothian coastline features extensive sand dunes and wide sandy beaches and is well-appreciated on the route between **Aberlady & Gullane [23]**, with a return inland along the John Muir Way.

Cramond Harbour

A selection of excellent paths and quiet country roads link the pretty village of Cramond with the peaceful surrounds of Dalmeny Estate via the River Almond, which played a central role in the industries that developed at Cramond during the 18th and 19th centuries. Three iron forges and two steel furnaces worked the river, with steel and iron exported as far afield as India. Heading further back into history and a chapel was built here in 600AD and then Cramond Kirk, with the earliest part of the building dating back to the 1400s.

The beautiful River Almond Walkway bookends this walk, which begins beside the attractive little Cramond Harbour. Follow Riverside past Cramond Boat Club onto the River Almond Walkway. A path proceeds through woodland, in due course passing more houses and a car park onto another woodland path. Beyond an old stone building and an impres-

sive weir, climb a flight of steps and continue above the river.

Ascend another steep flight of steps high above the River Almond, then descend back to the riverside path. At a fork go right, continue to Dowies Mill Lane, turn right and walk to Braepark Road. Turn right, cross the River Almond over the impressive Cramond Brig (which is around 700 years old and in remarkable condition) onto Cramond Brig Toll.

Climb uphill and just before reaching the A90 turn right onto a track sign-posted for Queensferry. Follow this round a gate into Dalmeny Estates from where a fine track (Cycleway 76) progresses through attractive country-side. Once past East Craigie a narrow road continues for 750m. As the road swings left go straight on around a gate and descend a rough track into wood-land. At a fork bear left and drop down to Eagle Rock where a path signposted 'Shore Walk' turns left (an indistinct

START & FINISH: *Cramond Harbour (NT189771)*

DISTANCE: *12km; 7.5 miles*

TIME: *3hrs 30mins*

MAP: *OS 65*

TERRAIN: *Road, tracks & paths*

GRADE: *Easy/Moderate*

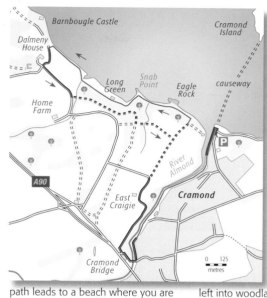

Drum Sands and at a pocket of pine woodland it bears right to run above a beach. Just before reaching woodland leading to Barnbougle Castle, turn left then left again onto an estate road.

The road climbs past the wonderful Dalmeny House, which is the family home of the Earls of Rosebery. It was completed in 1817, having been designed by William Wilkins, who also designed the National Gallery in London. At a crossroads turn left, follow an estate road southeast and at a fork go

path leads to a beach where you are only a stones throw from Cramond).

Follow the shore walk past Snab Point, and by several secluded beaches. Eventually the path reaches a narrow road beside Long Green. Go straight across onto a woodland path. Beyond a footbridge the path runs alongside a golf course beside the broad swathe of

left into woodland. At the next fork go right onto a rougher track which climbs steadily out of the woodland, then swings right to a crossroads. Turn left and follow a rough road back to the outward-bound route. Retrace your steps over Cramond Brig then along the River Almond Walkway back to Cramond.

The Ochils from Cramond

Silverknowes

Over the causeway to Cramond Island

Cramond causeway at high tide

Cramond translates from Gaelic as Fort of the Almond, indicating a history that extends back some 2000 years. The Romans built a fort here between AD140 and AD142 near to the eastern extremity of the Antonine Wall, which ran between the Forth and Clyde estuaries and marked the north-western frontier of Roman occupation.

Today Cramond is an attractive and peaceful coastal village. Sitting just off the coast is Cramond Island, which can be reached at low tides by a causeway. Although uninhabited today, discarded hazelnut shells found on the island were carbon dated to 8,500BC and are thought to have been left by Mesolithic hunter-gatherers. During World War I and II Cramond Island was used as part of the Firth of Forth defences. The streets of Cramond offer pleasant walking with Lauriston Castle making for an interesting diversion.

If the tide allows, take the causeway from Cramond Harbour and follow this onto Cramond Island, where a selection of paths allow for exploration. There are fine views of Edinburgh and the Forth Rail Bridge.

Back on the mainland, turn left from the causeway and walk along Cramond

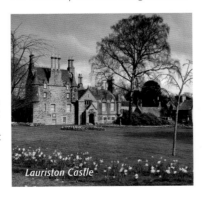

Lauriston Castle

START & FINISH: Cramond Harbour (NT189771)

DISTANCE: 11km; 6.75 miles

TIME: 3hrs 15mins

MAP: OS 66

TERRAIN: Road, tracks & paths

GRADE: Easy/Moderate

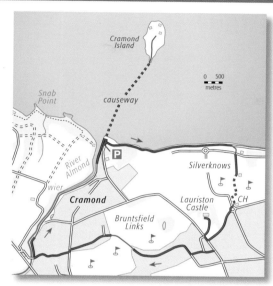

Lauriston Castle is set within an historic garden laid out by the great Scottish architect William Henry Playfair in the 1840s. Guided tours around the castle run from Saturday to Thursday between April and October and at weekends between November and March.

Retrace your steps back to Cramond Road South and turn left, then right onto Barnton Park. Walk along here by some very impressive villas to Barnton Avenue. Go right and follow the pavement, which eventually narrows to

foreshore, where there are lovely views along the coast to Granton. Follow the esplanade for approximately 1.5km and just before a little stand of pine trees, turn right and climb a grassy embankment to Marine Drive.

Go straight across onto a narrow road (still Marine Drive) and follow this through Silverknowes Golf Course, which enjoys superb views. Walk to the right of the clubhouse through a car park, then right at a roundabout onto Lauriston Farm Road and follow the pavement to Cramond Road South. Turn right and after approximately 100m turn right through a gate onto Lauriston Castle entrance drive.

Follow this to the impressive tower house, the oldest part dating from 1593, with a two-storey extension being added between 1824-27.

a path then runs in-between Bruntsfield Links and Royal Burgess Golf Courses.

The path soon gains Barnton Avenue West. Continue through the leafy suburbs of Cramond and at Whitehouse Road go straight across onto Braepark Road. Continue to Dowies Mill Lane, turn right and take this narrow road alongside the River Almond.

Once by a row of houses bear left onto the River Almond Walkway, which proceeds through mixed woodland. In due course steps ascend high above the river then two flights drop back to the riverside path, which then passes by an impressive weir and an old stone building. Once past some houses and a car park, the walkway continues through more woodland, exiting at Cramond Boat Club at Cramond Harbour.

Arthur's Seat

An iconic landmark with spectacular views

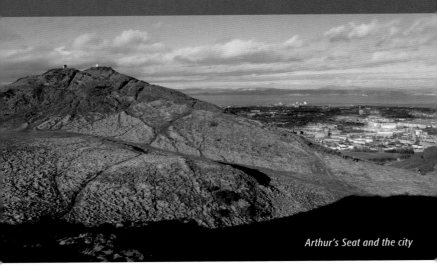

Arthur's Seat and the city

There can't be many cities with a volcano slap bang in the centre, but Edinburgh is one such place. Arthur's Seat dominates Scotland's capital and is a conspicuous sight for miles around. The underwater volcano that eventually formed Arthur's Seat was active until about 335 million years ago with glaciation then forming the profile we see today. Salisbury Crags, which circle the lower slopes of Arthur's Seat, also shaped the theories of renowned geologist James Hutton (who taught at Edinburgh University in the 17th century) regarding the age of the earth. Today a variety of paths climb over the crags and onto Arthur's Seat, granting some of the finest views in central Scotland.

Facing the Scottish Parliament on Horse Wynd, turn left and follow the road by Holyrood Palace into Holyrood Park, once the Royal hunting grounds of King David I. David built Holyrood Palace as an abbey in the 11th century but it later became the official Scottish residence of the British monarch, something which continues to this day. It was here in 1566 that Mary, Queen of Scots' husband, Lord Darnley, was brutally murdered by Mary's private secretary David Rizzio, instantly becoming one of the most notorious episodes in Scottish history. The palace is open daily except when royalty is in residence.

Follow the pavement to a roundabout. Turn right onto Queens Drive and at the next roundabout cross over and continue along Queens Drive. Soon bear left onto an obvious grassy path, which climbs gradually beneath Salisbury Crags' imposing cliffs, eventually gaining a red gravel path. Bear left and climb the path to the base of Salisbury Crags. Turn left onto the crags

START & FINISH: *Holyrood Park (NT264739)*

DISTANCE: *8km; 5 miles*

TIME: *2hrs 30mins*

MAP: *OS 66*

TERRAIN: *Tracks, hill paths & parkland*

GRADE: *Moderate*

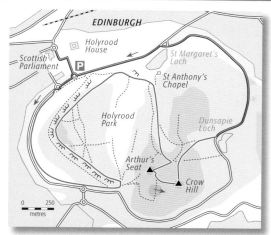

A quieter descent follows an obvious path east, which zigzags down onto flatter ground. Continue onto Crow Hill, then drop steeply north back onto Queens Drive. Turn left, follow the pavement by Dunsapie Loch to a junction at St Margaret's Loch. Turn left, walk through Holyrood Park back to Horse Wynd and return to the Scottish Parliament.

taking the centre of three paths, which hugs the lip of the cliffs and climbs to the summit – care should be taken as the drop throughout is exposed. The panorama of the Edinburgh skyline is incredible.

Descend east along the crags towards St Margaret's Loch. At a fork go right and beyond a tarmac path, at a prominent rockface, turn right onto a gravel path and climb steeply by the ruin of St Anthony's Chapel, thought to have been built around the 1300s as an outlying chapel for Holyrood Abbey.

A path from St Anthony's Chapel comes in from the left. Bear right onto this and climb steeply towards Arthur's Seat. It soon swings left beneath the summit onto a grassy plateau. Turn right and ascend a stony path, alongside a fence onto Arthur's Seat's airy 251 metre summit via some clambering over slabs of rock, which can be greasy when wet. Again the views are fabulous.

Salisbury Crags

Tropical Palm House

Port of Leith sits at the mouth of the Water of Leith and possibly, but maybe not surprisingly, translates from Cumbric, as 'Wet Place'. The original harbour was constructed in 14th century (subsequently becoming Edinburgh's main port) with the Victoria, Albert and Imperial docks being built between the 17th and 19th centuries.

Much redevelopment took place in the 1990s and today the Port of Leith is one of Edinburgh's cultural hotspots, as well as being the home of the Royal Yacht Britannia and the Scottish Executive (Scotland's Civil Service). This walk also visits the splendid Royal Botanic Garden Edinburgh. Originally founded in 1670 near Holyrood, it has been located at Innerleith since 1820, and its collection of plants from around the world makes it one of Edinburgh's top tourist attractions.

From the corner of Commercial Street and Shore, follow Shore to Sandport Place, bear right over the Water of Leith then turn left onto the Water of Leith Walkway, which runs for 12.5 miles to Balerno and is a wonderful way to cross Edinburgh – wildlife includes goldeneye, cormorant and kingfisher. The first section of walkway to Broughton Road follows the route of old railways which once connected the port with the rest of the city.

Walk along the wooded path to a junction, go left and pass underneath a road bridge. Stick to the main path underneath three more bridges, bear left at a fork then right at the next onto Warriston Path. Follow this, soon crossing the Water of Leith by a viaduct. At Broughton Road turn right, go right again onto Canon Mills, descend onto

START & FINISH: *Commercial Road & Shore (road) (NT271766)*

MAP: *OS 66*

DISTANCE: *10.5km; 6.5 miles*

TERRAIN: *Roads, tracks & paths*

GRADE: *Moderate*

TIME: *3hrs*

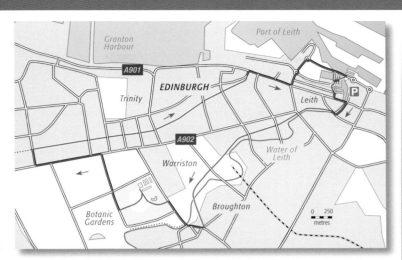

Innerleith Row and follow this a short distance to the East Gate entrance of the superb Botanic Gardens.

Turn left through the gate, bear right at the East Gate Coffee Bar then left to climb a path past the Rock Garden. At a junction turn right then go straight on at a crossroads past a pond, turning left at the next junction. Continue to the splendid Tropical Palm House, which was built in 1834.

Retrace steps a short distance to a fork. Turn right, climb the path, taking the next right and descend to the visitor centre at West Gate. Exit right onto Arboretum Place, continue along Arboretum Road and turn left onto Ferry Road. Walk by Stewart Melville rugby ground and just before a super-market turn right onto Pilton Drive. Once across a bridge, immediately turn left down steps onto the Ferry Road cycle/walkway.

Follow this lovely, peaceful path

(another former railway) for approxi-mately 2.75km, passing underneath a number of bridges. Once underneath Newhaven Road Bridge, turn left onto a path signposted for Newhaven Harbour. Turn right onto Hawthornvale, then right again at Lyndsay Road. At Ocean Drive, turn left then right at a roundabout. Follow Ocean Drive past Leith Docks and over a new bridge beside the conspicuous arched Victoria Swing Bridge which when built in 1874, was the largest swing bridge in the United Kingdom.

Turn immediately right back over the Water of Leith via the swing bridge to the new flats of Rennie's Isle. Follow a pedestrian route between the flats and the Scottish Executive building then turn left through a car park onto Commercial Quay. Turn left through an archway onto Dock Place then right back onto Commercial Street.

Portobello & Joppa
Edinburgh's best-known beachfront

Sand stabilising groynes, Portobello

ortobello is a charming coastal district, sitting a short distance east of Edinburgh's city centre. Prior to the late 17th century the coast was popular with seamen and smugglers and during this period a local sailor built a house here and named it Portobello, after the Battle of Puerto Bello in which he had been involved. In due course the town adopted the name.

Portobello reinvented itself during Victorian times as a spa resort, replacing Leith Sands as the preferred location for Edinburgh's middle classes to enjoy relaxing spas, water baths, sea and sand. It continued to grow in reputation with the arrival of the railway, bringing holidaymakers from further afield. This popularity with day-trippers and holidaymakers continues and the lovely coastline and bustling High Street provide contrasting focal points to this

inviting walk.

From the small car park on Bridge Street, turn right onto Portobello Promenade and walk above the beach or along the soft sand which is divided by several distinctive, wooden groynes. The promenade has fine views along the coast as far as North Berwick Law and is lined with some striking buildings and distinctive architecture, particularly the red sandstone façade of the Portobello Swim Centre, which dates from the Victorian era.

Continue to the eastern extremity of the promenade on the outskirts of Joppa. If walking along the beach leave it by a ramp or steps to join the promenade beside a bandstand. Turn left onto Musselburgh Road (B6415) and walk along the pavement into Joppa, where, invariably, the waves will crash into the sea defences. Joppa's unusual name is

START & FINISH: *Bridge Street car park Portobello (NT305743)*

DISTANCE: *7.5km; 4.5 miles*

TIME: *2hrs 10mins*

MAP: *OS 66*

TERRAIN: *Roads & beach*

GRADE: *Easy*

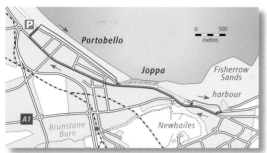

thought to have been taken in the late 18th century from a local farm, itself derived from the Hebrew word Yapho, meaning beautiful. The route soon passes by Joppa Pans, where salt was produced between 1630 and 1953 and Rock Cottage, which dates from the 16th century and is the oldest house in Portobello.

Continue through Joppa, to a set of traffic lights at the junction with Edinburgh Road (A199). Go straight on, towards Musselburgh, and once across a bridge over the Brunston Burn take the next left onto a side street (an off-shoot of Edinburgh Road) and follow this to Fisherrow Sands. Turn right and follow the lovely beach to reach Fisherrow Harbour, described in more detail in **Fisherrow & Prestonpans** [16].

Turn right from the beach, walk through a car park and turn right onto New Street. Follow this back to Edinburgh Road (A199), bear right and head away from Fisherrow, retracing your steps back to the promenade at Portobello Beach. Go straight on here onto Joppa Road (B6415) and follow the pavement by Abercorn Park, into Portobello. Walk back to Bridge Street along attractive Portobello High Street, which is home to many independent shops, cafes and restaurants and dominated by the impressive Town Hall, first opened in 1914.

Portobello promenade

*N*ewhailes is one of Scotland's finest stately homes and stands in beautiful parkland a few minutes from Fisherrow Harbour. The architect James Smith, heavily inspired by the Venetian architect Andrea Palladio, built the original house, named Whitehill, in 1686. However when Smith ran into financial difficulties Sir David Dalrymple bought it in 1707 renaming it Newhailes (Dalrymple also owned the ruined Hailes Castle near East Linton and would later be Solicitor General for Scotland and Lord Advocate).

Renowned architects William Adam and then William Burn extended the house with a library being built to house the Dalrymple's massive collection of books. The contents of the library are now in the National Library of Scotland, whilst Newhailes came under the care of the National Trust for Scotland in 1997.

This walk makes use of Newhailes extensive parkland and the surrounding countryside of Newhailes and Brunstane Burn. Facing Fisherrow Harbour, turn left onto New Street then right onto Edinburgh Road (A199). Cross the road bridge over the Brunstane Burn then turn left at a sign for the 'Brunstane Burn Walkway' where a riverside path runs to the right of the burn. Cross the burn again via a foot-bridge and follow the path right then left to a junction.

Go straight on along the path over another small footbridge then through woodland and countryside. Having passed under a railway bridge continue to Brunstane Road South. Turn right here then left onto Gilberstoun. Descend the tree-lined road past Brunstane Railway Station and then climb through a quiet housing estate,

START & FINISH: *Fisherrow Harbour (NT335729)*

MAP: *OS 66*

DISTANCE: *6.5km; 4 miles*

TIME: *2hrs*

TERRAIN: *Roads, tracks & paths*

GRADE: *Easy/Moderate*

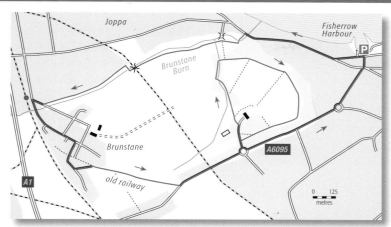

taking the third road on the right signposted for Gilberstoun Loan, Brig and Wynd.

Just before Gilberstoun Loan turn left through a gate onto a path. Follow this to a junction and here bear left onto a cycle/walkway (a dismantled railway), and follow it through open countryside to Newhailes Road (A6095). Turn left, walk along the pavement towards Musselburgh then, at a roundabout, turn left into Newhailes.

Once past a car park go left at a fork then follow the path to the right past the house and through the estate. Pass a path on the right then turn right at the next path, which enters attractive wood-land. Go left at the next fork and once a bridge over a burn is crossed, climb a flight of steps to another fork. Go right and continue to a waymark. Turn left, follow the path in-between woodland and a field. At the next fork turn left then right and follow a fenced path clockwise around the estate, with good views over Musselburgh, to a three-way junction.

Take the centre path into woodland (enjoying an abundance of wildflowers during spring and summer) bearing left at a fork and continuing back to the entrance drive. Exit Newhailes left onto the A6095 and descend into Musselburgh to a roundabout. Bear left onto Newhailes Road and at Edinburgh Road cross onto Harbour Road and return to Fisherrow Harbour.

Ramsons (Wild Garlic), Newhailes

16 Fisherrow to Prestongrange
Salt, fish & King Coal

Fisherrow Harbour

There has been a small port at Fisherrow on the Firth of Forth since the 16th century with the present harbour built in 1850. The port was at its busiest during the mid-19th century when a fleet of around 30 boats caught herring in the Firth of Forth. By 1950 the fleet was no more although many of the fishwives managed to find work at nearby Newhaven. Fisherrow Yacht Club, founded in 1957, now uses the harbour, which is the end (or starting) point of the John Muir Way (described in the last chapter).

Facing Fisherrow Harbour turn right onto the John Muir Way (JMW), which heads east along the seafront promenade above Fisherrow Sands onto a parkland path. Cross Mountjoy Terrace to reach the River Esk, turn right and walk along a lovely riverbank path, crossing the River Esk over a footbridge at New Street.

Turn left onto Goosegreen Crescent and follow the river onto Goosegreen Place. Go round a barrier, walk along a grassy path then bear left onto a track beside a JMW sign. Follow this above Fisherrow Sands and around to the right alongside a sea wall. Eventually a path bears right into Levenhall Links and crosses an area of grassland. Beyond a gate turn left onto a path. This runs alongside a park road to a gate. Go through the gate, turn right then left to the B1348.

Follow this beyond the right turn to Prestongrange Museum to a path on the right over old railway tracks, just before the brick museum building. The site has buildings and machinery associated with the former colliery and brickworks, plus exhibitions and a cafe.

Return to the main road and continue to the edge of Prestonpans where a JMW sign on the left indicates a tarmac path back through the parkland of

START & FINISH: *Fisherrow Harbour (NT335729)*

DISTANCE: *12km; 7.5 miles*

TIME: *3hrs*

MAP: *OS 66*

TERRAIN: *Road & paths*

GRADE: *Easy/Moderate*

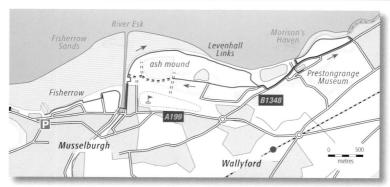

Morison's Haven. This section of reclaimed coast used to be one of Scotland's main ports, but is now a haven for meadow pipit, seals and goldeneye.

Just after an information board bear left onto a path, which returns to the B1348. Turn right, retrace your steps along the pavement, turning right then left, through a gate, back into Levenhall Links. At the next gate go straight on, cross an area of grassland, beyond which the path then skirts some woodland. Cross a track to reach the first of the ash lagoons. During the 1960s Levenhall Links was a disposal ground for ash from Cockenzie Power Station. In recent years lagoons have been landscaped and now form part of a nature reserve, home to the likes of skylark, redshank and tufted duck.

Walk along the lagoons' southern edge, veering right to a gate. Once through bear left onto a path and walk through scrubby grassland to a junction beside the steep embankment of an ash mound. Turn left and walk along a track to the left of the embankment, which offers some stunning views towards Edinburgh. Bear left at a fork then right at a crossroads and return to the outward-bound track at the mouth of the River Esk. Retrace your steps back to Goosegreen Place and over the River Esk to Fisherrow

Ash lagoon nature reserve

17 Musselburgh & the Esk
Home to mussels & the world's oldest golf course

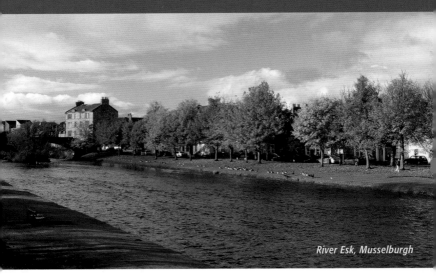

River Esk, Musselburgh

Having been inhabited since the Romans established a fort near to the mouth of the River Esk, Musselburgh is one of Scotland's oldest towns and the largest in East Lothian. Musselburgh prospered from the 17th century due to industries such as fishing (Musselburgh translates simply as 'mussel town'), wool and coal mining. Several fine bridges cross the River Esk at Musselburgh (the rebuilt Roman Bridge dates from 1597) whilst the eye-catching Tolbooth was erected in 1590. Musselburgh is also home to the oldest golf course in the world, thought to date from 1672, although it may be even older as Mary, Queen of Scots is said to have played here in 1567.

Facing The Tolbooth (now a café) on High Street (A199), turn left, then at Shorthope Street turn right, and walk to the River Esk. Turn left, follow a river-bank path beside Eskside East under the New Bridge at Bridge Street to join Mall Avenue and continue onto Olive Bank Road.

Cross the road just before a bridge, descend some steps, turn right onto Station Road and once by Eskmill House, bear right onto a riverbank path. Walk by some industrial buildings and then a weir, with the woodland path hugging the banks of the meandering River Esk where kingfisher and heron reside. Keep on the path as it passes some large houses at Inveresk Estate and then makes its way through open countryside to arrive at a public path on the left just before a railway bridge.

Follow this onto Wedderburn Terrace at Monktonhall and once across Carberry Road (A6124) walk along Pinkiehill Lane. Beyond a gate turn right onto Crookston Road and continue

START & FINISH: *The Tolbooth, Musselburgh High Street (NT347727)*

DISTANCE: *8.5km; 5.25 miles*

TIME: *2hrs 30mins*

MAP: *OS 66*

TERRAIN: *Road, tracks & paths*

GRADE: *Easy*

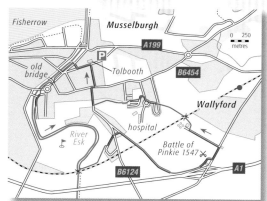

onto Pinkie Drive, cross Pinkie Avenue then bear right at a roundabout, passing Edenhall Hospital entrance. Turn left onto Edenhall Crescent and after a few metres bear right and follow a path over parkland, and through a housing estate into Lewisvale Park.

Walk through the park, exiting right onto Inveresk Brae (A6124). At Inveresk Road turn right then left onto Newbigging and return to High Street.

south-east, crossing a bridge over a railway line. A quiet country lane (bestowing fine views of the Pentlands) eventually narrows to a path, which climbs gently onto a road near the A1. Walk past a cottage and on to a monument commemorating the Battle of Pinkie.

This took place here on the 10th September 1547 and was the culmination of several years of Rough Wooing by Henry VIII, which commenced after the Scottish Government refused to allow Mary, Queen of Scots to marry Henry's son, Prince Edward (the government's preferred option for Mary was the Dauphin of France). The battle was a disaster for the Scottish Army with an estimated 6,000 deaths.

Turn left, descend Salter's Road (A6094) towards Wallyford, turning first left onto a public path for Pinkie and Musselburgh. Just before a gate beside an industrial site, turn right, follow a path underneath the railway line then descend through fine countryside onto Pinkiehill Crescent. Turn right then left

Musselburgh Tolbooth

Prestonpans mural

Prestonpans is labelled 'Scotland's Mural Town' due to the large, colourful and eclectic murals, painted by a variety of artists, that are located around the town, each depicting a different aspect of the town's heritage and culture. This includes the famous Battle of Prestonpans, which took place here in 1745, salt panning and mining (both key industries in the early development of the town), and famous people.

From the car park follow the John Muir Way (JMW) north-east round the coast behind Cockenzie Power Station with its two dominating chimneys. As Cockenzie Harbour is approached take a path right to Edinburgh Road, then right again to a mural on the wall outside the power station, depicting a procession based on the town's annual Gala Queen parade.

Continue into Prestonpans on High Street past an archway on the right, Sir Walter Scott Pend, which is home to a mural of Scott who, aged eight, was sent to the town in the hope that sea bathing would help improve his lameness. Keep along High Street passing a stone shelter with a painting of Robert Burn's greatest work, Tam O' Shanter.

High Street contains a number of striking, and beautifully illustrated murals, including one of John Muir (the Dunbar born father of modern conservation), Morison's Haven Harbour, portraying the coal, salt and fishing industries and the wonderful Prestongrange Totem Pole, which celebrates over 1,000 years of Prestonpans and the barony of Prestoungrange. Also on High Street is The Gothenburg, a great pub and restaurant, which has several murals within its walls.

Continue out of Prestonpans for about 800m to the end of the wall, fence and trees on the south side of the B1348. Cross carefully to old

START & FINISH: *Edinburgh Road car park (NT391751)*
DISTANCE: *10km; 6.25 miles*
TIME: *3hrs*

MAP: *OS 66*
TERRAIN: *Roads & paths*
GRADE: *Easy/Moderate*

railway tracks and a path into woodland, to the left of a wooden fence.

Follow the path to more old tracks and swing right alongside them, passing old rolling stock and mine buildings, part of the superb open-air Prestongrange Museum. Turn right onto a road, then right again and through a large gate to an access road which leads left to the museum building. The museum is open from April to October 11.30am to 4.30pm and admission is free; there are several murals here as well.

Continue on the road to just past the museum where a path beside an old metal footbridge leads through woodland and over railway tracks back to the main road. Cross over with care and walk right to a JMW signpost. Turn left here and follow the road past a small car park towards the sea to a path skirting Morison's Haven, to emerge back on the main road just before Prestonpans.

Turn left then right into Prestongrange Road and follow the pavement past Cuthill Park (where there are more murals and is worth a quick diversion) climbing gently to a roundabout. Turn left onto the B1361 and walk through the upper part of Prestonpans, all the way to Johnnie Cope's Road. Cope was in command of the government forces at the Battle of Prestonpans and was defeated by Bonnie Prince Charles' Jacobite army. Turn right to Prestonpans Railway Station and its 100 Thousand Welcome's mural.

Retrace your steps back to the B1361, go straight across and descend Station Road (passing the fine Jacobite mural), swinging left then right onto West Loan, continuing by Preston Tower, a striking 14th century keep, back to High Street. Turn right and follow High Street. Just before a small park on the left which is overlooked by Prestongrange Kirk, turn left to gain a slipway on the shore and follow it right to a path leading back to the car park.

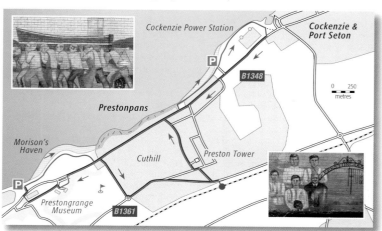

Seton Sands at dawn

A combination of beachfront promenade, woodland paths and beach link the East Lothian towns of Cockenzie, Port Seton and Longniddry. Both Cockenzie and Port Seton merge imperceptibly and are dominated by the coal-fired Cockenzie Power Station. From the late 16th century onwards coal has figured in Cockenzie's history. Cockenzie Harbour was utilised to export the coal from nearby Tranent and it also became a centre, like many other settlements along the coast, for salt panning.

Port Seton grew from the nearby hamlet of Seton during the 1600s and in 1656 the 11th Lord Seton built Seton Harbour. Port Seton then grew, primarily as a fishing village. Coal mining and weaving played a role in the early life of Longniddry but it wasn't until 1916, when the Scottish Veterans' Garden Cities Association built 20 cottages for veteran's injured in World War I, that the village developed.

Facing Cockenzie Harbour climb steps on the right, walk through a small car park then go straight on and follow the John Muir Way above Cockenzie shore to emerge on Wemyss Place at Port Seton Harbour. Turn left , walk along Viewforth then bear left through the railings and down steps to the lovely little harbour and follow it round onto a promenade. Follow this alongside Links Road (B1348) past Wrecked Crags and Long Crags, to eventually swing right to Links Road.

Turn left and follow the pavement above gorgeous Seton Sands, which has been popular with holidaymakers since the early 20th century. Once past Seton Sands Caravan Park bear left at a John Muir Way signpost and walk along the beach passing Longniddry Bents No.1 car park. Once past No.2 car park bear right and cross a footbridge to reach the B1348.

Carefully cross the road round a wooden barrier onto a public right of

START & FINISH: Cockenzie
Harbour (NT398757)

DISTANCE: 10km; 6.25 miles

TIME: 3hrs

MAP: OS 66

TERRAIN: Roads, paths & beach

GRADE: Easy/Moderate

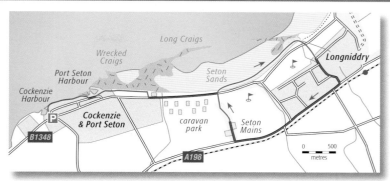

way, which crosses Longniddry Golf
Course – keep an eye out for golfers
and golf balls. Exit the course around
another barrier onto a lane and follow
this straight onto Links Road.
Continue south into the appealing
surrounds of Longniddry village. Upon
reaching Main Street (A198), turn right
and walk past some of the attractive
red-roofed veteran's cottages then
continue out of Longniddry and along
a dual carriageway towards Seton
Mains.

Turn right, walk along a road towards
the small number of distinctive houses
of Seton Mains. Bear right at a fork from
where a red gravel track passes by
more cottages. Turn left onto a narrow
path into peaceful Seaton Dean
Woodland and follow this back towards
the coast. In due course it runs to the
left of Longniddry Golf Course, then
passes through a gate onto a lane.
Keep along this to the B1348 beside
Seton Sands Caravan Park.

Carefully cross the road, turn left and
retrace steps back to Cockenzie
Harbour, enjoying fine views north
across the Firth of Forth and west to
Edinburgh.

Port Seton harbour

53

20 Longniddry to Aberlady
A linear walk along the John Muir Way

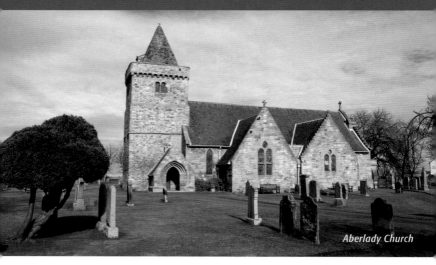

Aberlady Church

The coast between Longniddry and Aberlady, highlights the exceptional, and sometimes rare, variety of wildlife that thrives along the Lothian and Berwickshire shoreline. Longniddry Bents is a Site of Scientific Interest, due in no small part to a number of water voles that inhabit the burns and red-necked grebes that visit the coast between November and March. Chiffchaff, willow warbler, reed bunting, redshank, and curlew can also be spotted at different times of the year whilst grey seals are regularly seen.

Contrasting sharply with the wildlife are the remains of World War II tank traps at Longniddry, which were erected as protection against enemy invasion. Many of these concrete blocks are now hidden amongst the coastal grassland. The return journey from Aberlady to Longniddry can be made by either retracing steps or by using the excellent bus service that runs between Aberlady and Seton Sands.

From Longniddry Bents No.1 car park, turn right onto Seton Sands and walk north-east along a beautiful section of soft sand, soon passing by the entrance to No.2 car park. Once across a wooden footbridge a sandy path travels around a rockier section of headland and then along a sea wall beside the B1348.

Follow the path through dune grass, enjoying fine views along the Firth of Forth. After crossing a burn via a foot-bridge go left when the grassy path splits and continue by Ferny Ness until Longniddry Gosford Car Park is attained. Walk all the way through the car park, exiting onto a broad track and bear right at a fork into a pocket of woodland beside the A198. Once out of the woodland the path runs along a sea

START: *Longniddry Bents No. 1 car park (NT431762)*
FINISH: *Aberlady (NT465799)*
DISTANCE: *5.5km; 3.5 miles*
TIME: *1hr 30mins*

MAP: *OS 66*
TERRAIN: *Road, paths & beach*
GRADE: *Easy*

wall around the broad sweep of Gosford Bay.

At a fork go left, walk through another pocket of woodland and then through coastal grassland, passing the entrance of Gosford Estates. The path crosses a wooden footbridge then meanders through a lovely section of oak, beech and Scots Pine woodland towards Aberlady. Once across the entrance for Green Craig, the path runs alongside Craigielaw Golf Course, crossing its entrance drive and Wemyss and March Estates, as well as the entrance to the Scottish Ornithologists' Club. Open to the general public, the centre houses the George Waterston Library, the largest collection of ornithological reference books and journals in Scotland, and the Donald Watson Gallery where exhibitions by many leading wildlife artists and photographers are held throughout the year.

A pavement then continues into the centre of Aberlady village, passing Aberlady Kirk en route. This lovely building dates from the 15th century, and its two burial aisles from the 16th and 17th centuries. The church's origins date back to the 8th century, with links to early Christian centres at Iona and Lindisfarne. Aberlady Kirk is open daily between April and October and subject to request at other times of the year.

Pentland Hills from Longniddry

Cottage on Gosford Estate

Sitting on the outskirts of Aberlady, Gosford Estate was purchased by the Wemyss-Charteris family in 1781. At this point the family began to plant woodland and set out ponds and pleasure gardens. The gardens today include several listed buildings such as the boathouse and mausoleum and the woodland paths grant some beautiful, tranquil walking.

The centrepiece of the estate is Gosford House. Work began on this magnificent stately home in the late 18th century to a design by the great Scottish architect Robert Adam. However Gosford House wasn't completed until 1800, eight years after Adam's death.

In 1808, Francis Charteris 8th Earl of Wemyss, removed the house's two wings, but they were reinstated in 1891 by his grandson (also Francis), the 10th Earl. Internally Gosford House is equally elaborate, particularly the magnificent Marble Hall.

The house is open to the public on various days throughout the year <www.gosfordhouse.co.uk> and an annual permit can be bought from the Wemyss & March Estate Office or the Gosford Bothy Farm Shop (£5 at the time of writing), which grants unlimited access to the estate policies.

The estate is accessed from the A198 via a minor road leading to Gosford Bothy Farm Shop & Cafe. This turning is directly opposite the access road to Wemyss & March Estate Office. There is unsignposted parking in the field on the left at the very start of the access road. Please do not park at the shop. From the parking follow the road down past the farm shop and its car park, continuing straight ahead through a gate onto a woodland track with a walled garden to the left.

The track swings right then left onto a single-track road and continues past a couple of beautiful cottages. From here it wends through more woodland to a fork. Bear right to reach the impressive Charteris Family Mausoleum, its pyramidal top particularly striking. Although the mausoleum has room for 64 coffins, it holds the remains of only one person, the 7th Earl of Wemyss,

START & FINISH: *Gosford Estate car park (NT457795)*
DISTANCE: *3km; 1.75 miles*
TIME: *1hr*

MAP: *OS 66*
TERRAIN: *Tracks & paths*
GRADE: *Easy*

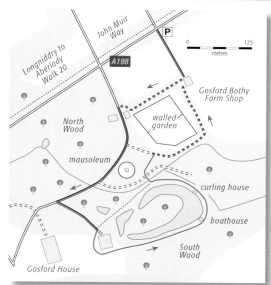

Walk past the estate buildings then turn left onto a path and follow this to the gorgeous environs of Gosford Lake, lined with a selection of beautiful trees, where swans, ducks, heron, dragonflies and damselflies reside and where time can easily be wiled away.

A grassy path travels anti-clockwise around the pond, swinging left by the old boathouse and the distinctive, 19th century Curling House which was used to store curling stones and equipment. Continue to a fork, turn right where a boggy path crosses a footbridge. Pass by tracks on the left then right and at a junction turn right. Follow a track to the right of the walled garden, swinging left to a gate. Beyond this, turn right onto the outward-bound road at the farm shop and walk back to the start.

another Francis Charteris.

Continue along the estate road, over a bridge and just before two large stone gateposts, turn left onto a narrow road, which continues through more woodland and a gate to reach some estate buildings with the stunning Gosford House to the right.

Gosford House

*A*berlady is a lovely village sitting at the edge of Aberlady Bay. The name possibly translates as River Mouth of the Lady (lady perhaps pertaining to The Virgin Mary) from the Pictish 'Aber', meaning river mouth, and the Old English word for lady, 'hlaedig'. There was an active harbour at Aberlady from 1149 and it was one of the few places in the vicinity where larger vessels could get close enough to the shore to load and unload, although this declined during the 19th century as bigger boats required deeper water.

The economy of the village was supplemented in the 1700s by weaving and also by illegal undertakings such as smuggling. Kilspindie Golf Course was laid out in 1876 and this walk follows the coastal edge of the course and around Craigielaw Point where there are some superb views of Edinburgh and the Pentlands.

From Aberlady follow Main Street (A198) towards Aberlady Bay. As the road swings right go straight on along a single-track road towards Kilspindie Golf Club. As a large stone house is reached go straight on by Kilspindie Golf Club car park, pass by the house and follow the road through a gate and by another small car park. Pick up a grassy path, which immediately forks. Go right where it follows the edge of the golf course, bearing left to head west around the rockier shore of Aberlady Point. Pay due heed to golfers on this section, keeping a lookout for balls and trying not to interfere with play. Stick to the path, which in due course passes a lovely red-tiled roof stone hut and continue beside the course, enjoying superb views of Arthur's Seat and Edinburgh, to reach a green at Craigielaw Point. The path bears left

START & FINISH: *Aberlady*
(NT465799)

MAP: *OS 66*

DISTANCE: *5km; 3 miles*

TERRAIN: *Road, paths & beach*

TIME: *1hr 30mins*

GRADE: *Easy*

Gosford Sands

around a green and drops down onto a lovely sandy beech. Walk south along the soft sand, beneath a bank of dunes towards Green Craig hotel.

At a wooden sea defence bear left from the beach onto a dune path, which skirts the edge of the golf course, to reach a low fence near the hotel.

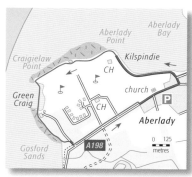

Cross this and turn left. Follow a path bearing right at a fork, and walk by the hotel, alongside another fence. This then gives way to a high wall at Harestanes Wood, with the path running above the rocky Gosford Sands and past concrete sea defences.

As a rocky section of Gosford Sands is approached, the path turns left through a gap in the wall from where an indistinct path heads through Harestanes Wood, passing in-between another line of concrete blocks and then alongside a burn to arrive at the Green Craig driveway. Turn right, cross a stone bridge and follow the drive for approximately 100m towards the A198.

Just before the road turn left onto a broad, woodland path and follow this north-east past Craigielaw Golf Course and the Scottish Ornithologists' Club — see **Longniddry to Aberlady** [20] — back into Aberlady.

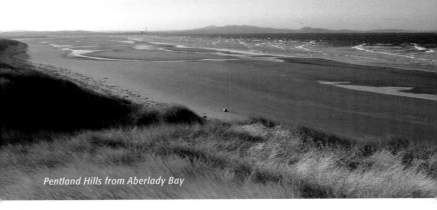

Pentland Hills from Aberlady Bay

Aberlady Bay was designated Britain's first local nature reserve in 1952 and is also a Site of Special Scientific Interest, due to the coastline's flora, fauna and geology. Sanderling, pink footed geese, lapwing, redshank, reed bunting, skylark, common blue butterfly, birdfoot trefoil and yellow flag iris are just some examples of the wildlife visible during this walk. Paths and tracks lead all the way into Gullane with a section of the John Muir Way returning to Aberlady Bay. Scottish historian and author Nigel Tranter also enjoyed this exquisite landscape, walking along Aberlady Bay every day as he wrote.

From the car park at Aberlady Bay, cross the wooden bridge over the Peffer Burn into the nature reserve. A good path heads north along Aberlady Bay through lovely coastal grassland. After a little pocket of woodland the path passes to the right of Marl Loch and continues to reach a convergence of paths beside Gullane Golf Course.

Take the left path (signposted Footpath) and follow this as it skirts the edge of the golf course. After another 200m the path forks again. Go left and follow the path as it climbs over dunes then drops down onto a beach a little before Gullane Point. Turn right and walk along this superb stretch of sand, then over a little shelf of rock to Gullane Point.

From here a path climbs onto the dunes and travels around Gullane Point to where it splits. Bear left, then right at the next fork, then left at the next. Continue east along the dunes onto a track and over a little beach from where an obvious path bears right and climbs steeply onto Hummell Rocks. Pass by some concrete blocks and go straight on to follow a broad grassy track at the edge of the golf course.

Climb to a wooden post and a narrow path on the left. Follow this high above the coast with fine views along Gullane Bents, to where the path forks. Walk right and then left onto a broader track,

START & FINISH: *Aberlady Bay (NT472805)*

DISTANCE: *8.5km; 5.25 miles*

TIME: *2hrs 45mins*

MAP: *OS 66*

TERRAIN: *Road, paths & beach*

GRADE: *Easy/Moderate*

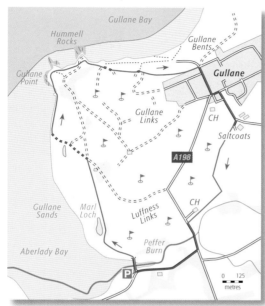

Turn left then right onto Saltcoats Road. As it turns right at Templar Place, go straight on and follow a single-track road, turning right when reaching the John Muir Way. At the next waymark bear right, pass through a gate and after a further 20m, beside a dismantled railway, go right at a fork.

Pass through another gate and follow a path to the left of Luffness Links, through scenic countryside, passing near to the ruin of Saltcoats Castle, an old tower house dating from the 16th century. The remains sit on a salt

then at a signpost for Gullane Bents turn left and descend a grassy path above a car park onto Marine Terrace. Immediately turn right onto Sandy Loan and continue into Gullane town centre at Summerside Place.

marsh, hence the name. The path eventually passes Luffness Links Clubhouse and goes through a gate to gain the A198. Carefully cross the busy road, turn left and along the pavement back to Aberlady Bay.

Bridge over the Peffer Burn

Gullane to Dunbar

Ravensheugh Sands

7he soft gentle sweep of the East Lothian shoreline between Gullane and Tyninghame is best known for its golf courses, particularly Muirfield, which has held the Open Championship on several occasions. But there is also a plethora of great walking along the coast and adjacent countryside and, as in the previous chapter, the superb John Muir Way is used to good effect.

Having passed through Gullane (pronounced Gullan) and Dirleton's charming ambience, next stop is the busy town of North Berwick, home to East Lothian's most conspicuous land-marks; North Berwick Law and Bass Rock. Castles at Tantallon and Dirleton are also popular visitor attractions, whilst beaches such as Broad Sands

and Ravensheugh are two of the finest stretches of sand to be found along Scotland's east coast. Several lovely pockets of woodland in and around Tyninghame add to the variety of walks in this chapter.

Walking Around Gullane Town [24] provides a great means to get under the skin of this fascinating and attrac-tive little town – Gullane Hill also grants one of the finest panoramas along much of the Lothian and East Lothian coastlines. Gullane Bents [25] takes you through the dunes past one of the UK's top golf courses, whilst the stun-ning walk between Gullane & Yellowcraig [26], overlooked by Fidra (the island was made famous by Robert Louis Stevenson), explores a glorious expanse of beach and some

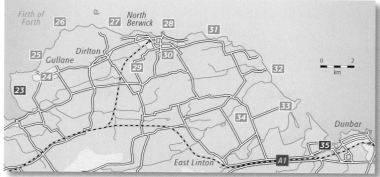

fine coastal paths and tracks, with an inland return on the John Muir Way via Dirleton.

Fidra is again a dominant feature of the route east from Yellowcraig to North Berwick [27]. Like route 26, this also utilises a variety of coastal paths with a return along part of the John Muir Way, to make this walk one of the most appealing walks in the chapter.

North Berwick is a great base from where several days of walking can be enjoyed. North Berwick & Milsey Bay [28] shows off all the town has to offer whilst the beach and glorious countryside from Broad Sands to Kingston [29] illustrates the diversity of walking here. North Berwick & The Law [30] offers one of the best views in Scotland. Although only 187m (613 feet) in height, North Berwick Law presents a breathtaking panorama across the Firth of Forth to Fife and over East Lothian to Edinburgh and the Pentland Hills. By way of contrast, the route between Canty Bay & Tantallon Castle [31] sticks to the coast but offers some tough walking. Canty Bay is a beautiful secluded beach and the ruins of Tantallon Castle one of the icons of the East Lothian coast.

The final three walks in this chapter start from the popular Tyninghame Estate at the western end of Belhaven Bay. Again there is a magnificent diversity of walking here; this is evident when exploring the amazing stretch of sand between Ravensheugh & Seacliff [32], which is another of East Lothian's fantastic secluded beaches, or when strolling round Sandy Hirst [33], a spit of sand and shingle formed by circulating tides at the mouth of the River Tyne. A simple walk around the peaceful sanctuary of Binning Wood [34] provides a fitting end to the walks in this chapter.

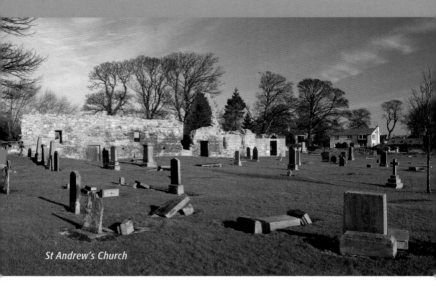

St Andrew's Church

Although Gullane's origins stretch back to the 9th century, it is only in the last century or so that this charming town has prospered, principally as a top golfing location. Golf has been played here since 1854 and today four courses surround the town (Gullane No.1, 2 and 3 and Luffness Links) whilst Muirfield, which has hosted The Open Championship 16 times, most recently in 2013, and is the oldest organised golf club in the world, sits on the outskirts of Gullane.

The town's population has grown from 230 residents in 1790 to the present day figure of nearly 4,000 and many of the town's fine houses date from the Victorian era when the tourist, and golfing boom began.

This walk makes use of the paths and pavement that surround Gullane and begins at The Smiddy, the town's oldest building. Facing The Smiddy on Main Street, turn right, walk through Gullane passing the remains of St Andrew's Church. A church was established on this site during the 800s, being replaced during the 12th century and it is thought that sections of the church survive from this time.

Turn right onto West Links Road and walk along the edge of Gullane No.1. Turn right onto Hummel Road then left onto Whim Road. A pavement climbs gradually, turning first right, from where Whim Road swings left to a gap in a wall. Go through here and climb a grassy track to reach the Millennium Cairn on Gullane Hill, where the panorama extends over much of East Lothian, Fife and Edinburgh.

Retrace your steps towards the wall but turn left just before it and walk past

START & FINISH: *Gullane, Main Street (NT488830)*

DISTANCE: *4.5km; 2.75 miles*

TIME: *1hr 15mins*

MAP: *OS 66*

TERRAIN: *Roads, tracks & paths*

GRADE: *Easy*

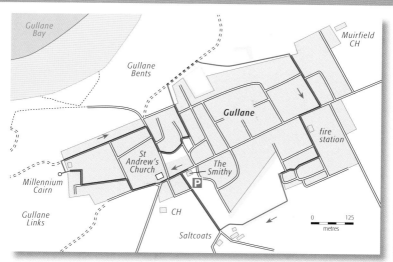

Golf & Gullane

a large sandstone house to a gate on the right giving access to Hill Road. This quiet road descends steeply by some fine villas. Turn right onto Sandy Loan and at Goose Green Road go left and walk along here to the left of parkland. The road turns left then right to gain Marine Road, which is followed up left to Marine Terrace.

Go straight ahead onto a grassy path to join a gravel track and follow it right-wards for approximately 50m to a gate on the right. Go through here and immediately fork left where a path cuts diagonally across grassland, then beside some houses. Beyond a pocket of Scots Pine turn right through a gate onto Muirfield Park and follow the pavement past several side streets back to Main Street.

Cross Main Street, turn right then left onto Muirfield Drive, walk past a fire Station, and turn right onto Muirfield Terrace which is followed over Muirfield Crescent to a park. Turn left, walk along the left edge of the park into Millennium Wood. A path veers right and runs through the strip of woodland, exiting onto a park path, which passes a large white house onto a practice golf area. Cross this onto a single-track road, turn right and follow it onto Saltcoats Road back to The Smiddy.

Gullane Bents

One the most popular beaches on the Lothian Coast

Gullane Bents & beach

Gullane Bents, 'bents' being a term used to describe an area of coastal grassland, plays host to a wide variety of fauna and fauna including roe deer, redshank, birdfoot trefoil, wild thyme, the ubiquitous buckthorn, reed bunting, small heath and common blue butterflies.

During World War II, Gullane Bents were heavily used for military manoeuvers, destroying the vegetation cover. After the war the dunes were resculpted and planted with marram grass and sea buckthorn to stabilise them and create today's 'natural' landscape. The remains of concrete tank trap blocks and fortifications, both for training and defence, can still be seen at many locations between Gullane and Aberlady

From Gullane Bents car park walk back towards the access road and cross the grass eastwards above the bay, past wooden benches to a gravel track. Turn left and follow the track away from the houses to where it becomes first a gravel and then a sandy path through the scrub and pine covered dunes.

Continue to where the path starts to descend and divides. Turn right here and continue beside a fence to skirt a marshy section via boardwalks, then ascend over dunes to another junction. Turn sharply right beside the wooden fence to follow it, then old metal fence posts marking the boundary of Muirfield Golf Gourse, to reach a large green barn and an area of felled and re-planted woodland.

Keep straight ahead to the second main path junction, turn left and descend towards the established pine trees (known as Jamie's Neuk), then

START & FINISH: *Gullane Bents car park (NT477831)*

DISTANCE: *6km; 3.75miles*

TIME: *1hr 45mins*

MAP: *OS 66*

TERRAIN: *Tracks, paths & beach*

GRADE: *Easy/Moderate*

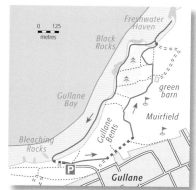

right before reaching them onto a path leading to a wide grassy track along the forest boundary towards the coast. Remain on this track to join a stony track leading down to the shore at Freshwater Haven.

Wander north-east round the sandy beach to rock platforms which offer a pleasant spot for a picnic, before returning south back along the beach to gain the coast path.

Assorted paths, both on the seashore and slightly more inland on the dunes,

lead past the remains of the 16th century St Patrick's Chapel to the eastern end of Gullane Bay. The chapel isn't the ruined stone building and wall near the start of the path, named the Red House on the 1853 Ordnance Survey map, but lies deeper into the scrub on the edge of the woodland further south.

Gullane beach is three kilometres long and very popular during the summer months thanks in part to its accessability and gently inclined sand, which offers excellent paddling and swimming water without great depth and no excessively strong currents. Like much of the Firth of Forth–North Sea coast, Gullane Beach can be windswept, although this makes it very popular with wind and kitesurfers.

Gain Gullane beach as soon as you can and follow it round to just before the sweep of sand is broken by the rocky outcrops of the Bleaching Rocks. Turn inland here to an obvious path by a lifebelt which ascends away from the beach to become a track leading to the public toilets, from where a tarmac road leads back to the car park.

Freshwater Haven

Gullane beach from the south

Sandy beaches, golf courses and an impressive ruined castle are the main features of this diverse route, which links the inland John Muir Way with well-established coastal paths. The walk also passes the island of Fidra, which is adorned by a fine lighthouse, see Yellowcraig & North Berwick [27].

From Gullane walk east along Main Street (A198) out of the town to reach a stone gatehouse on the left on the edge of woodland, after approximately 1.8km. Go through the wooden gate, signposted John Muir Way, onto a path through a pleasant strip of woodland, then through fields to meet the Archerfied Golf Links access road. Follow this left and straight on for 20m, then right onto a section of old road beside the southern boundary of the golf course. This leads to a gate and the attractive village of Dirleton,

dominated by the picturesque remains of Dirleton Castle.

The castle was built in the 13th century and served as the residence of the de Vauxe, Haliburton and Ruthven families until Oliver Cromwell's army destroyed it in the 1660s. Today the castle grounds are best known for their wonderful gardens and are open all year except Christmas and Boxing Day.

Turn left onto Manse Road, continuing straight ahead onto a track through fields, when the road turns right to houses. In due course swing right along the field edge, skirting woodland to a John Muir Way sign. Turn left then right and continue through woodland to a junction beside Yellowcraig car park.

Turn left, follow a broad track to Broad Sands, with the craggy island of Fidra and her lighthouse ahead. Just before the beach bear left, follow a

START & FINISH: *Main Street, Gullane (NT488830)*

DISTANCE: *11.5km; 7 miles*

TIME: *3hrs*

MAP: *OS 66*

TERRAIN: *Roads, tracks & paths*

GRADE: *Easy/Moderate*

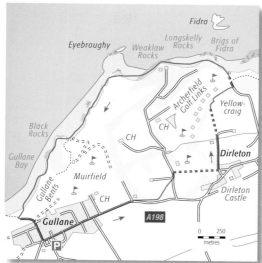

lovely views east to Fidra. Nearing the end of the beach bear left onto a path, which runs around a rocky headland and along the coast to cross another magnificent secluded arc of sand.

Follow this to its end, turn right onto narrow path, walk by the remains of an old house and wall, and continue as the path veers left around a beautiful sandy bay and then Black Rocks. Once across a short, rocky path, drop down onto Gullane Bay and walk along this stunning stretch of golden sand, beside the impressive dune system of Gullane Bents, with the houses of Gullane beyond.

path around the Brigs of Fidra and then drop down onto a beach. Another path is then picked up, which travels along Longskelly Rocks.

Just before Wreaklaw Rocks bear right down a sandy path then turn left and walk over a narrow rocky shelf (at high tides crossing here could be problematic) then west over a wonderful ribbon of sand, underneath sand dunes, with

Follow the beach for approximately 750m then bear left and climb a path to reach Gullane Bents car park beside an information board. Turn left, walk through the car park and follow the access road up to Sandy Loan, which is followed back into Gullane.

Gullane countryside

27 Yellowcraig to North Berwick
Broad Sands & Treasure Islands

*Broad Sands &
North Berwick Law*

The woodland, grassland and coastline linking Yellowcraig and North Berwick offers tremendous walking with good paths and tracks crossing diverse terrain. There are fine views throughout, particularly those of the chain of four islands positioned off the coastline. Bookended by the familiar sights of Fidra and Bass Rock are Craigleith and The Lamb. Both are home to important bird colonies with puffins, cormorants, razorbills, guillemots and herring gulls breeding there, whilst on Craigleith a pair of peregrine falcons has taken up residence in recent years.

Fidra has a ruined chapel and its lighthouse, built in 1885, is said to have been the inspiration for Robert Louis Stevenson's Treasure Island. Spending much of his early life in Edinburgh, Stevenson visited the East Lothian coastline on a number of occasions, and it is easy to see why such beautiful scenery inspired him.

From Yellowcraig car park walk along a track towards Fidra but before reaching the beach turn right at a John Muir Way sign onto a path. Follow this past public toilets, turn right at crossroads and continue by some magnificent old twisted trees to a waymark. Walk right here where the path leads through coastal grassland to a gate. Go through into woodland and beyond another gate follow a path diagonally across a field. Turn left at the next waymark, pass through another gate onto a narrow path, which travels alongside the perimeter wall of Invereil House. Pass through one more gate to reach Abbotsford Road on the outskirts

START & FINISH: *Yellowcraig car park (NT516856)*

DISTANCE: *7.5km; 4.5 miles*

TIME: *2hrs 40mins*

MAP: *OS 66*

TERRAIN: *Roads, tracks & paths*

GRADE: *Easy/Moderate*

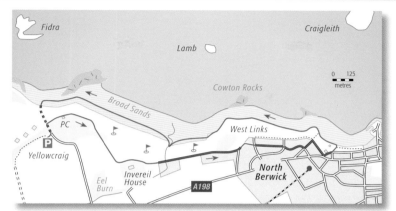

of North Berwick.

Turn left and follow this alongside North Berwick West Links Golf Course to its end, turning left onto Strathearn Road. Follow this onto a path, which swings right and continues beside a children's golf course and through a couple of gates to Upper Kaimend. Turn right then left into Cromwell Road, then over Fidra Road to York Road, and left onto Links Road. Walk by Inchgarry House (one time home of Dorothy Campbell, 1909 British and US Ladies Amateur Champion), to Pointgarry Road and follow this to the North Berwick West Links clubhouse. Turn left into Beach Road to reach a tarmac path beside a statue of Ben Sayers. Sayers was a successful golf professional, course designer and equipment manufacturer who lived in North Berwick until his death in 1924.

Follow the path across the grass and past the golf club starter's hut, then go left onto a grassy path above the sandy beach to gain the edge of North Berwick West Links, and stunning coastal views to the islands of Lamb and Craigleith. The path becomes sandier as it traverses over Cowton Rocks and then drops down onto the beautiful Broad Sands. Walk along this superb sandy beach, keeping close to the dunes to avoid rockier sections of the beach. In due course a footbridge crosses over the Eel Burn from where fine beach walking continues towards Yellowcraig, with fantastic views of Fidra. Once opposite Fidra, turn left from the beach onto an obvious, sandy track. Walk along here onto a firmer track and follow this back to Yellowcraig car park.

Fidra

28 North Berwick & Milsey Bay
Promenading on the Lothian Riviera

North Berwick

*N*orth Berwick's history stretches back to the 12th century when the town developed around its harbour. A ferry service used to leave North Berwick and cross the Firth of Forth to Earlsferry in Fife and was a popular shortcut for pilgrims heading to St Andrews. North Berwick's two broad sandy beaches helped it grow as a fashionable holiday resort during the Victorian era, and this popularity continues to this day. This walk utilises both beaches and explores much of this bustling and attractive town.

From the Scottish Seabird Centre walk by St Andrews Old Kirk then turn left onto Melbourne Road. It is thought a church has stood here since the 5th century with St Andrews Old Kirk being built around the 1100s. It became an important place of worship for both locals and pilgrims until much of it was destroyed by a storm in 1656.

Bear left onto Milsey Bay and walk east by Milsey Rocks. At its eastern edge bear right to the top of the beach onto a sandy path, which climbs steeply up a grassy slope to gain a higher path. Turn right then left up two flights of steps to reach Haugh car park, granting a wonderful view of North Berwick.

Cross the car park through a gate onto Glen Golf Course. Follow a grassy path as it swings right along a fairway and around a green onto a track, which exits the golf course onto Lime Grove. Pass some distinctive red-roofed cottages then take the second road on the right. Turn left at Rhodes farmhouse onto a path signposted 'The Beach'. This descends gently to the edge of Glen Golf Course. Turn left onto a tarmac path, walk by some houses, then bear right at a fork.

Descend steps and then continue alongside the golf course, crossing a footbridge. Turn right onto a path beside an old ruined cottage and just

START & FINISH: Scottish Seabird Centre (NT554857)
DISTANCE: 5km; 3 miles
TIME: 1hr 30mins

MAP: OS 66 & 67
TERRAIN: Roads, paths & golf course
GRADE: Easy

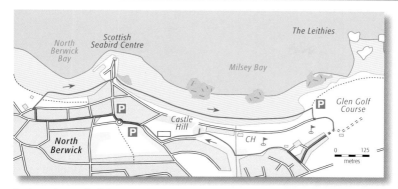

before Glen Golf Club car park, turn left and continue through North Berwick Glen. At the last house bear left, climb a steepish path, then turn right onto the superb viewpoint of Castle Hill. This was a strategic stronghold during the 13th and 14th centuries when the Lauder family (who were local landowners) erected a tower here, but later abandoned it for the securer strongholds of Tantallon Castle and Bass Rock.

From Castle Hill retrace your steps past the outward-bound path then turn right and follow a paved path, which runs alongside Glasclune Gardens. Turn right down steps and past tennis courts, then turn left onto East Road beside Quadrant. Go along East Road, turn right onto Quality Street, then left onto High Street. Follow High Street to West End Place and turn right down that to Beach Road. Go left then right onto a tarmac path and past a statue to Ben Sayers, see Yellowcraig & North Berwick [27], to gain North Berwick Bay. Turn right, walk along this fine stretch of sand past the harbour and climb the slipway back to Melbourne Road and the Seabird Centre.

Milsey Bay from the east

North Berwick Harbour

Although North Berwick is primarily known for its coastline and beaches the countryside surrounding its western and southern fringes is equally scenic, particularly the quiet country roads near Kingston, which provide gorgeous views of East Lothian.

From the Scottish Seabird Centre cross Victoria Road, then bear right down a slipway onto West Sands. Follow this west alongside North Berwick Golf Course, and then hug the line of the dunes around Cowton Rocks onto Broad Sands. As a steep, sandy embankment is reached, bear left from the beach, cross a burn by a wooden footbridge then turn right and continue towards Yellowcraig, with the island of Fidra and its prominent lighthouse ahead.

When directly opposite Fidra, turn left from the beach onto a wide, sandy path and head south onto a firmer path to approach Yellowcraig car park. Just before a gate turn right at signpost for Dirleton and follow a woodland path, turning left then right at the next waymarks. The path soon bears left away from the wood and crosses a field to gain Manse Road. Follow this into the attractive village of Dirleton, home to the historic Dirleton Castle, see Gullane & Yellowcraig [26].

Turn left from Manse Road to reach Dirleton Road (B1345) and follow this east out of the village past the post office to Station Road, opposite open fields on the edge of the town. Turn right and follow this to the A198. Carefully cross this busy road from where Station Road continues south-east through beautiful, open countryside towards Kingston.

START & FINISH: *Scottish Seabird Centre (NT554857)*
DISTANCE: *13.5km; 8.25miles*
TIME: *4hrs 30mins*

MAP: *OS 66*
TERRAIN: *Roads, tracks, paths & beach*
GRADE: *Easy/Moderate*

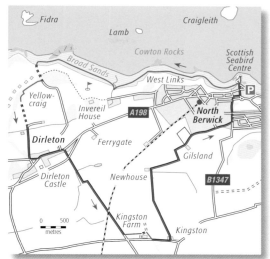

left, turn right at a waymark and follow a field edge to a gate. Go through the gate, turn left and walk along a narrow path beside a quiet road into Kingston.

Take the first road on the left, and walk north along this country road, which grants outstanding views of East Lothian, Fife, and the Pentlands. Continue by Newhouse Farm and Gilsland Caravan Park (with superb views of North Berwick Law) for approximately 2.5km

Pass under a railway line and then after approximately 500m (and just before a road junction), turn left through a gate onto a signposted foot-path along a field edge by Kingston Farm, to pick up a farm track. Bear left and follow the track but as it swings to Grange Road on the outskirts of North Berwick and follow this past several side roads to gain Law Road. Turn left and descend back into North Berwick. Turn right onto High Street, then left onto Quality Street, and back to the Seabird Centre.

Countryside around Kingston & North Berwick Law

30 North Berwick & The Law

A steep climb to a spectacular viewpoint

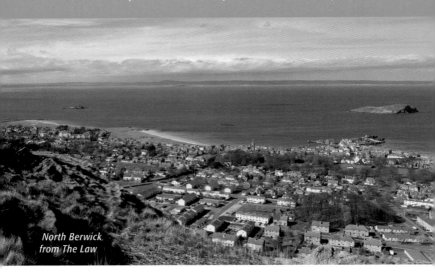

North Berwick
from The Law

The 187 metre volcanic plug of North Berwick Law is an eye-catching prospect along much of the Lothian and East Lothian coast-line and a climb onto her conical summit grants one of the finest panoramas in the region. Formed by volcanic activity around 300 million years ago, North Berwick Law is also in sight of other dormant volcanoes such as Fife's East and West Lomond, and Arthur's Seat above Edinburgh.

As it rises from the low-lying coastal landscape, North Berwick Law has, for many years, been used as a watch station and the derelict buildings on the summit are relics from the Napoleonic Wars and the Second World War. A gentle climb through the busy streets of North Berwick lead to the base of North Berwick Law from where a short, but very steep, climb, along good paths, concludes at the exposed summit. The exertion required is very much worth the effort.

From the Scottish Seabird Centre walk south along Victoria Road onto Quality Street and then swing right onto Kirk Ports passing by The Lodge, which was built in the 18th century as a dower house and is now the oldest inhabited house in North Berwick. Sitting adjacent to The Lodge is Walltower House, which was built by Sir Hugh Dalrymple in 1747, and subsequently extended as a town house for his family, who were local landowners and a prominent family within the town.

Continue along Kirk Ports by the substantial remains of The Parish Kirk, which dates from 1664, and was built as the successor to the original North Berwick Parish Church. Turn left onto Law Road and follow it past North Berwick Sports Centre to Law Primary School. Turn left onto Lochbridge Road

START & FINISH: Scottish
Seabird Centre (NT554857)
DISTANCE: 5km; 3miles
TIME: 2hrs

MAP: OS 66 & 67
TERRAIN: Roads, tracks & paths
GRADE: Easy/Moderate

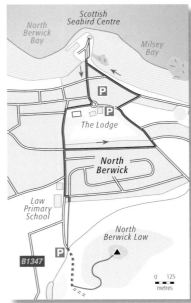

Scottish Seabird Centre

North Berwick Bay

Milsey Bay

The Lodge

North Berwick

Law Primary School

North Berwick Law

B1347

0   125
metres

then immediately right onto Wishart Avenue, from where a path leads through a car park at the base of North

Berwick Law, to an opening in the wall beside a gate.

Go through and bear right to a path around the lower slopes of North Berwick Law. At a signpost for North Berwick Law turn left and climb a steep path. It is a tough pull although it soon levels out. At this point take a stony path on the left, with steep ground again being covered, and some fine views beginning to open out. The path then bears right to climb steeply through craggy outcrops, passing the old watchtower ruin, to gain the summit. The views are breathtaking with Bass Rock, Tantallon Castle and the islands of Craigleith and Lamb being particular standouts.

Retrace your steps back through the car park at the base of North Berwick Law onto Haddington Road. Descend Law Road turning right onto St Baldred's Road and then left onto East Road. Walk back towards North Berwick town centre, turning right onto Quadrant then left onto Melbourne Road and walk above Milsey Bay back to the Seabird Centre.

North Berwick's old Parish Kirk

31 Canty Bay & Tantallon

East along the coast to an iconic castle

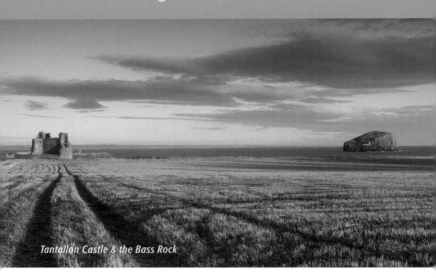

Tantallon Castle & the Bass Rock

Lying east of North Berwick is little Canty Bay. There is only one (private) road leading to it, whilst the walk from North Berwick described below has some rougher terrain to cross, making Canty Bay a slightly awkward place to get to. However it is a delightful, peaceful spot with sumptuous views of Bass Rock.

This walk also visits the fascinating remains of Tantallon Castle, which dates from the 1350s and was built by William Douglas from distinctive local red sandstone. The Douglas family was one of the most powerful in Scotland and Tantallon Castle came under siege many times, finally succumbing to Oliver Cromwell's marauding army in 1651. Now under the care of Historic Scotland, Tantallon Castle is open daily. There is an admission charge.

From the Scottish Seabird Centre walk east along Milsey Bay passing by Milsey

Rocks. At the end of the beach bear right onto a sandy path, which climbs steeply to a junction. Go straight on through a gap in a wall, turn left and follow a path through grassland, with Glen Golf Course to the right. The path swings right to run east above the coastline, until it drops steeply to continue along some sandy bays around the rocky peninsula of The Leithies. Stick to the top of the beach as lower down the terrain is rocky. A little climbing over boulders is required to gain a grassy embankment beside a golf green. A path then heads by another bay to a fork beside a stony beach. Go left, cross the beach around Leckmoram Ness, eventually arriving at Canty Bay. Pick your way through rockier ground underneath steep cliffs onto Canty Bay's gorgeous arc of sand.

Walk along the beach towards some houses. En route some slabs of rock

START & FINISH: *Scottish Seabird Centre (NT554857)*

DISTANCE: *10.5km; 6.5 miles*

TIME: *3hrs 30mins*

MAP: *OS 66 & 67*

TERRAIN: *Roads, tracks, paths, beach & golf course*

GRADE: *Moderate/Strenuous*

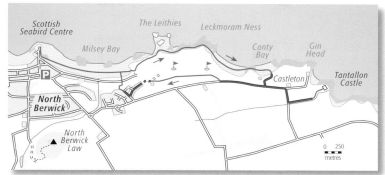

have to be negotiated, which can be a little awkward and hands may be required. Back on the sand continue past the houses and after a wooden cottage turn right from the beach then right onto a track. A narrow road then climbs steeply to the A198. Walk left on the pavement then, with care, along a grass verge for about 200m, to reach the access road to Tantallon Castle.

Retrace your steps along the A198 (during the summer the verge is lined with wild poppies) passing Canty Bay cottages. At the edge of Glen Golf Course, before some trees and a row of red-roofed cottages, turn right through a metal gate onto the course.

Bear left and walk along its left edge (taking great care of flying golf balls and observing good golf etiquette), descending gently past a caravan park then bearing right around the back of a green.

Turn left onto a red gravel path and follow this onto Lime Grove. Pass some distinctive red-roofed cottages, take the second road on the right then turn left at Rhodes farmhouse onto a path sign-posted 'The Beach'. This leads back to Glen Golf Course, from where a fenced path drops down some steps. Cross a single-track road back to Milsey Bay, turn left and walk along the beach back to the start.

Tantallon Castle

Ravensheugh Sands is a dazzling stretch of white sand, more reminiscent of Scotland's celebrated west coast. It is where the monk St Baldred arrived in the 8th century, becoming the first recorded settler at Tyninghame. He then established a monastery and built a small chapel on Bass Rock, embarking on many retreats to the island, where it is also said he ended his days.

Ravensheugh Sands culminates at the beautiful secluded cove of Seacliff, which grants fantastic views of both Bass Rock and Tantallon Castle, perched precariously on cliffs nearby. Seacliff is also home to Britain's smallest harbour. It should be noted that at high tides, the rocky section of Scoughall Rocks may be impassable.

Walk through Tyninghame Links car park passing a 'path to beach' signpost. Go through a gate onto a woodland track and follow this south-east towards the shore. At a fork go left and follow the path through a line of large concrete blocks. Upon reaching an old wall continue to a gate. Turn right where a broader track soon leaves the woodland onto scrubby grassland to reach the rocky shelf of St Baldred's Cradle and a large red sandstone seat.

Bear left here and walk north-west along a grassy then sandy path. At an information board descend onto the golden expanse of Ravensheugh Sands, relishing wonderful views of Bass Rock. A couple of burns will cause no problems at low tide but at higher tides may mean getting your feet wet.

Once past Peffer Sands, the route over Scoughall Rocks crosses stones and larger rocks and can be awkward in places. Continue by a series of secluded coves, containing some interesting geological features. Once through an obvious gap between two crags, pass round the headland by St

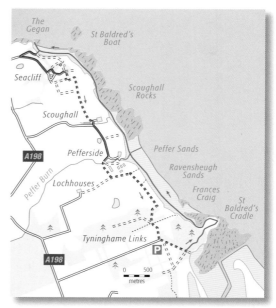

START & FINISH: *Tyninghame Links car park (NT627809)*

DISTANCE: *12km; 7.5 miles*

TIME: *3hrs 30mins*

MAP: *OS 67*

TERRAIN: *Roads, tracks, paths & beach*

GRADE: *Moderate/Strenuous*

Bass Rock from Seacliff

Baldred's Cross to Seacliff and walk along the sand to The Gegan and seek out Britain's smallest harbour.

Retrace your steps about half way along the top of the beach and climb a flight of wooden steps to a small car park. Turn right, follow a single-track road and once around a barrier turn left onto a minor road. Just before a cottage fork left, follow the road past an archway and turn left at the next fork.

The road now proceeds through open countryside. At a crossroads turn right onto a track and skirt the woodland to reach a track on the left which is followed beside a wall. Pass through a gap on the right and continue south to Scoughall. Just before some buildings turn right onto a road and at the next junction turn left around a gate. Continue south on another road through Pefferside crossing the Peffer Burn over a footbridge on a rougher track. Turn left at the crossroads east of Lochhouses, go round a gate and follow a track towards the dunes, swinging right at a signpost for Tyninghame Links. The track heads south-east alongside the dunes into woodland. At a fork turn left, pass through a gate and walk back to Tyninghame Links, going through a final gate to the car park.

33

Sandy Hirst

A short excursion into the River Tyne

Tyne Sands

Sandy Hirst, the little spit of land that stretches south from the woodland and coastline at Tyninghame, has been formed over many millennia due to a combination of the River Tyne entering the bay here and circulating tidal flows. Sandy Hirst is surrounded by a number of different landscapes, ranging from woodland, beach and salt marsh to mudbanks, dunes and coastal grassland.

Because of this diversity of habitats the wildlife to be found is equally varied. Wood anemone, wood sorrel, red clover, red campion, sea pinks and common spotted orchid are a selection of flora that thrive here at different times of the year. Butterflies and dragonflies are frequent summer visitors whilst over 200 species of bird have been recorded including whooper swans, wild geese, little egret, whimbrel, greenshank, oystercatcher,

sandpiper, dunlin, knot, curlew and golden plover. There are also fine views during the walk making Sandy Hirst a wonderful spot to sit and linger. It should be noted that at very high tides the beach at Sandy Hirst may be impassable.

From Tyninghame car park follow the track past Ash Road North to a junction of paths. Go straight on through a gate and walk along a bridleway lined with wildflowers during spring and summer, which runs south-east through mixed woodland. Keep straight on until the rocky shore at Tyne Sands is gained where there is a wonderful view towards Dunbar.

When the path splits turn right and walk along the shoreline, skirting woodland to the right. In due course the path veers left onto the low-lying finger of Sandy Hirst. Depending on the height of the tide either walk along the

START & FINISH: *Tyninghame Links car park (NT627809)*

DISTANCE: *4.5km; 2.75 miles*

TIME: *1hr*

MAP: *OS 67*

TERRAIN: *Tracks & paths*

GRADE: *Easy*

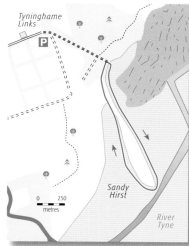

enjoying fine views across the water to the northern tip of John Muir Country Park. The beach then runs to the left of woodland and rounds the southern tip of Sandy Hirst. Again fine views extend across the outflow of the River Tyne to Hedderwick Plantation and beyond to the low, rounded hills of East Lothian.

Walk around the headland (with the distant outline of Traprain Law above East Linton particularly eye-catching) and then continue north. Here the landscape is markedly different with coastal grassland and mudbanks dominating. Keep to the edge of woodland and in due course a more defined path is picked up, which then heads through dune grass.

Eventually the path returns to the woodland at the southern edge of Tyninghame, which in turn leads back to the outward-bound path. Turn left here and retrace steps along the woodland track back to the car park.

sandy shore or keep to the coastal grassland at the top of the beach. Make your way south along the eastern shore in the company of wading birds,

Sandy Hirst &
the River Tyne

34

Binning Wood
A peaceful woodland walk

Near Lochhouses

*E*asily navigable paths and tracks travel through the woodland and countryside of Tyninghame and into Binning Memorial Wood. Although the majority the trees are around 60 years old, having been replanted after World War II, the original Binning Wood dates from the early 1700s when it was planted by Thomas Hamilton, 6th Earl of Haddington, on his family estate of Tyninghame.

Much of the timber was felled between 1942-45 and used in the production of Mosquito fighter-bombers during World War II. Today, part of Binning Wood has been set aside as a green burial ground, with caskets and coffins made from biodegradable materials to minimise the environmental impact on this gorgeous woodland sanctuary.

The striking red sandstone of Tyninghame House stands a little south-west of the starting point. It was built in 1829 to a design by the Edinburgh architect William Burn although there was a manor house on the estate from as early as the 11th century, and was used as a country residence for the bishops of St Andrews during the 13th century

Walk through the car park past a metal gate on the left then turn left through a gap in a fence onto a wide track. Follow this in a northerly direction, keeping right at a junction and descend through broadleaved woodland, which is soon left behind. The track then swings left and runs beside the dunes backing Ravensheugh Sands, then turns left again to pass by several strips of pine woodland. Go through a gate onto a rough track and keep left (right goes to Pefferside) with expansive views across a broad sweep of agricultural land to the cone of North Berwick Law and Bass Rock's flatter outline.

Keep on past several lovely red-tiled buildings at Lochhouses onto a single-track road, which veers left then right past some farm buildings (watch out for traffic) and then continues through a lovely rural landscape, with the conspicuous tip of Whitekirk Church to the north-west. Walk along the road

START & FINISH: *Tyninghame Links car park (NT627809)*
DISTANCE: *9.5km; 6 miles*
TIME: *3hrs 10mins*

MAP: *OS 67*
TERRAIN: *Roads, tracks & paths*
GRADE: *Easy/Moderate*

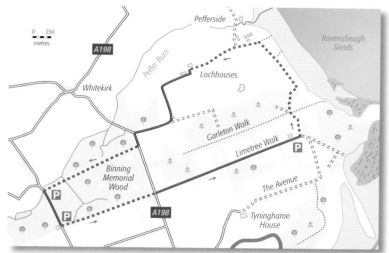

until the A198 is gained.

Carefully cross here then turn left. After approximately 200 metres turn right through a wooden gate into the lovely Binning Memorial Wood. A wide

Binning Wood

track proceeds west through predominantly beech woodland (the tree canopy is stunning during the autumn) where a broad variety of wildlife resides. Walk along the track for 1.25km and exit through a gate and pass a small car park.

Turn left, where a minor road travels south-west alongside Binning Memorial Wood. When opposite East Lodge, turn left through another car park and a gate back into the memorial wood. From here another excellent track proceeds along its southern fringes, cutting a straight course back to the A198, again exiting through a gate.

Carefully re-cross the road onto the long, straight Limetree Walk access road and follow this for just over 1.5km back to Tyninghame Links Car Park. There is a fine view of the red castellated towers of Tyninghame House en route.

Dunbar to St Abbs's Head

Victoria Harbour, Dunbar

Dunbar is the largest town on the East Lothian coast, but as you head south-east towards St Abbs and into the Scottish Borders, the coastline becomes increasingly rugged and the landscape more open. The geology is dazzling and the beaches and cliffs an ideal habitat for a mind boggling display of birdlife.

Dunbar of course was the birthplace John Muir, naturalist, explorer and father of modern conservation, and the John Muir Way starts a short distance down the coast at Dunglass. Several walks in this chapter make use of the path, passing places such as Catcraig, Barns Ness and Skateraw. Part of the Southern Upland Way, which reaches its eastern extremity at the lovely little village of Cockburnspath, is also utilised when walking in and around Cove and Pease Bay.

Dunbar & John Muir [35] are both celebrated in this superb walk which goes west from the town to John Muir Country Park, home to over 400 species of flora and fauna. Dunbar itself has many fine buildings (including the remains of Dunbar Castle), an absorbing history, two scenic and historic harbours and a lovely beach, all of which are visited when walking **Around Dunbar [36]**.

Several out and back walks exploit the 14.5km of the John Muir Way between Dunbar and Dunglass, where the coastal path grants fine views and lots of wildlife. **Dunbar to Barns Ness [37]**, **Catcraig to Skateraw [38]** and **Thortonloch to Dunglass [39]** take in a variety of historical sites including Barns Ness Lighthouse built by the family of Robert Louis Stevenson, Torness Nuclear Power Station opened in 1988, and the 15th century Collegiate Church at Dunglass.

The route round **Dunglass Mains [40]** allows Dunglass Collegiate Church to

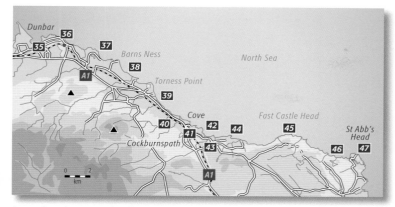

be explored in more detail utilising the local paths which link it with Cockburnspath. This village is also the start point for a further two walks. Picturesque and historic Cove Bay is the focus for first route from **Cockburnspath to Cove** [41], while the second reverses a section of the Southern Upland Way between **Cove & Pease Bay** [42], with a return through Pease Dean Nature Reserve and past Cockburnspath Tower back to the start.

The aforementioned **Pease Dean** [43] is owned by the Scottish Wildlife Trust and supports a magnificent range of flora and fauna. From Pease Bay a great walk passes the ruined St Helen's Church and along cliffs to the geological spectacle at **Siccar Point** [44], where James Hutton, doctor, lawyer, farmer and father of modern geology, confirmed his theory of the age of the earth in 1788.

Fast Castle [45] sits perilously close to the edge of the rocky Fast Castle Head but grants a dramatic and historic focal point for this short but tough walk. Spectacular cliffs are also a feature of the last two walks in the chapter. The route round **Coldingham Loch** [46] takes in the high cliffs west of St Abb's Head, utilising a new section of the coastal path, while the hike round the National Nature Reserve of **St Abb's Head** [47] offers stunning scenery and a wildlife watcher's paradise.

Descending to Dowlaw

Dunbar coast

John Muir Country Park is named after John Muir, naturalist, explorer and regarded by many as the father of modern conservation, who was born in Dunbar in 1838. Although he moved to the USA aged 11, his formative years spent in Dunbar may have sown the seeds of his ideas and ideals. The John Muir Country Park is a fitting legacy to the man who established the concept of National Parks and contains over 400 species of plants as well as kittiwake, skylark, meadow pipit and ringed plover, amongst many other birds.

From Dunbar High Street turn right down Victoria Street then left onto Victoria Place to Victoria Harbour. Walk left along the harbour, go left at a fork onto a path, which climbs around the front of Dunbar Leisure Centre. Go straight through the car park, turn right down a flight of steps onto the John Muir Way and walk west along the coast. Descend then ascend some steps then turn left up more steps, pass through a stone archway, ascend another flight of steps and turn right onto an esplanade. Follow this to its end, turn left down two flights of steps where a path skirts the edge of Winterfield Golf Course, turning south along Belhaven Bay. Just before some wooden chalets, go right at a fork, descend to Shore Road and go straight on at a junction. Shore Road turns left after a car park to reach a waymarked path on the right.

Walk beside Belhaven Bay then swing left along the Biel Water. Cross a bridge over the river, turn right, and walk north-west through coastal grassland into John Muir Country Park. At a fork go left then right before a car park. At the next fork go straight on (leaving the JMW) and walk north-west then south-west along Hedderwick Sands, and around Hedderwick Plantation to its

START & FINISH: *Dunbar High Street (NT679789)*

DISTANCE: *12km; 7.5 miles*

TIME: *3hrs 30mins*

MAP: *OS 67*

TERRAIN: *Roads, tracks & paths*

GRADE: *Moderate*

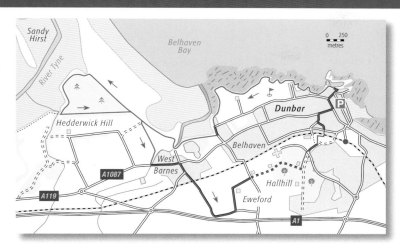

western perimeter.

Go right at a fork then turn left at a junction onto the JMW near a foot-bridge crossing the RiverTyne. Follow a path east, along Hedderwick Plantation's southern edge back to the outward-bound track. Turn right, and once past the car park, leave the JMW and go straight on. A public path crosses a field then proceeds alongside the River Biel to the A1087.

Turn left, and, after 250m, turn right and climb School Brae onto a minor road. Cross a railway bridge and walk down this quiet road to a scattering of houses at Eweford. Turn left, along a narrow road past Eweford Farm to a junction. Continue straight ahead on a track to woodland, eventually reaching a junction beside Lochend Cottage, a little north of Hallhill.

Follow the path onto Kellie Road. Go straight over and through a car park keeping right of Hallhill Sports Ground to a fork. Walk left by a football pitch,

turn right then left through a railway underpass. Cross Countess Road onto Countess Avenue, then right onto Countess Crescent to emerge opposite Dunbar Library. Turn right and follow Delisle Street back to the High Street.

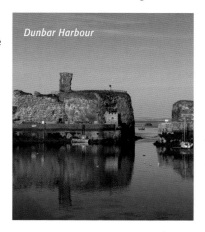

Dunbar Harbour

Around Dunbar

Historic harbour town

Cromwell Harbour, Dunbar

Dunbar is probably best known as the birthplace of John Muir, but the town has a history that extends back around 2,000 years. At this time a fort was built where the remains of Dunbar Castle stands today, and over the subsequent centuries the castle became one of the most important in Scotland. Due to its location near to both Edinburgh and the Scottish/English border, Dunbar prospered as a port from around the 14th century onwards, with the Victoria and Cromwell harbours becoming focal points for trade. Today Dunbar is an attractive town built around its bustling High Street and is home to many interesting buildings (some with close links to Muir), several of which are passed on this walk.

From Dunbar Railway Station, walk along Station Road, turn left onto Countess Road then right onto Abbey Road. Follow this onto High Street, turn left and walk by the striking 16th century Town House, which is now a museum. Outside stands a fine statue of a young John Muir.

Turn left onto West Port and after 50m go left through a stone archway to the remains of Dunbar's Trinitarian priory, established by Christiana de Brus, Countess of Dunbar in the 1240s. Retrace your steps to High Street and follow it left past the excellent John Muir Birthplace Museum (open Mon-Sat, Apr-Oct and Wed-Sat, Nov-Mar), then bear left onto Bayswell Road passing the impressive red sandstone façade of Lauderdale House. This was built in 1740 for local MP, Captain James Fall, and later extended by architects Robert and James Adam. Turn right from Bayswell Road through a pair of stone pillars, walk down steps and right onto the John Muir Way. Walk by Dunbar Leisure Centre, turn left and descend a path to Victoria Harbour,

START & FINISH: *Dunbar Railway Station (NT681785)*

DISTANCE: *4km; 2.5 miles*

TIME: *1hr*

MAP: *OS 67*

TERRAIN: *Roads, paths & beach*

GRADE: *Easy*

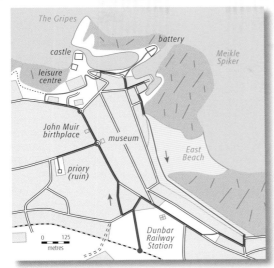

along the lovely sand to the very end of the beach then turn right at a John Muir Way sign onto Golf House Road then right onto East Links Road. Follow this in-between two red brick walls until the left one ends, then climb a grassy path up a steep embankment onto Queens Road (A1087). Turn right, walk by Dunbar Parish Church and the war memorial, turn left onto Countess Road then left onto Station Road to return to the start.

which is overlooked by the remains of Dunbar Castle.

Walk along the quayside away from the castle and bear left after the RNLI station over the iron swing bridge to the old artillery battery on Latimer Island, built after an American ship attempted to attack the harbour in 1781. Return over the bridge and keep straight ahead into Victoria Place, then left onto Victoria Street, which culminates at the picturesque Cromwell Harbour. This centers round the east pier, repaired in 1656 after storm damage via a grant from Oliver Cromwell's government and subsequently associated with him.

Turn right, follow the quayside around the harbour onto Shore Street then turn left onto Cromwell Haven. Once past some colourful houses bear left down a ramp onto East Beach. Walk

John Muir statue

37 Dunbar to Barns Ness

Stevenson lighthouse on the North Sea coast

Storm clouds gathering; Barn Ness Lighthouse

The coastline between Dunbar and Barns Ness is rocky, jagged and extremely picturesque. The most extensive limestone outcrops in central Scotland are found along much of this coast and, as well as limestone, other sedimentary rocks include sandstone, mudstone and coal. All were formed in the early Carboniferous, some 360 million years ago and were deposited in clear, warm seas where coral reefs existed – fossils found include corals, sponges and plants.

This geology fascinated the renowned geologist James Hutton during the 18th century and he formulated many of his ideas regarding the age of the earth from the rocks and fossils found here, see Siccar Point [44]. A short geological trail runs from Catcraig to Barns Ness, providing further details of the geology at Barns Ness. The John Muir Way path clings to this wonderful

coastline, providing an invigorating walk, particularly when strong winds whip waves in from the North Sea.

From Victoria Harbour walk along Victoria Place and turn left onto Victoria Street, to reach the Cromwell Harbour. Walk to the right along the quayside onto Shore Street then turn left onto Cromwell Haven. Once by some colourful houses bear left down a ramp onto the East Beach.

Walk along the lovely sand to the very end and onto a promenade above the rugged coastline. A path then continues to the left of Dunbar Golf Course clubhouse and car park from where it follows the coastal edge of the course – keep an eye out for golfers and golf balls. Once across a stone bridge over a burn, the course narrows and the path crosses another bridge over the wider Brox Burn.

Bear left from here and stick to the

START & FINISH: *Victoria Harbour, Dunbar (NT680793)*
DISTANCE: *10.5km; 6.5 miles*
TIME: *3hrs 30mins*

MAP: *OS 67*
TERRAIN: *Roads, tracks & paths*
GRADE: *Easy/Moderate*

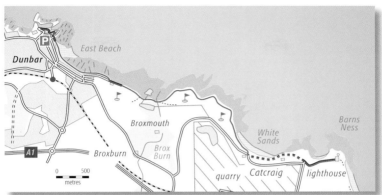

coastal edge of the course with the prominent marker of Barns Ness Lighthouse coming into view. To the right, beyond a wall sits Broxburn where Cromwell's English Parliamentarians and the Scottish Covenanters, led by David Leslie, met at the Battle of Dunbar in 1650.

Continue past a stone shelter with the path then becoming a little rougher underfoot as it passes around the gorgeous White Sands. The golf course is left behind with the path continuing through marram grass. In due course it swings right then left onto an access road at Catcraig. Follow this through a small car park then climb to a gate where the geology trail begins.

A stony track passes the remains of a limekiln, which were prevalent here during the 18th and 19th centuries and important to the local economy. Within the kilns layers of coal and lime-stone were burnt to create lime, which was spread onto the local fields (it was also exported to Aberdeen) to create, for many, the finest soil in Scotland. The last kiln closed in 1921. Continue

along the track then bear left onto a grassy path and follow this along the geology trail to Barns Ness lighthouse – see **Barns Ness to Skateraw [38]**.

From Barns Ness retrace your steps back to Dunbar enjoying superb views to Bass Rock and Dunbar en route.

Barn Ness

The coastline between Catcraig and Skateraw Bay is well away from any roads or major settlements and so a quiet and revitalizing couple of hours can be spent walking the coastal paths between the two points. This beautiful little bay sits in the shadow of Torness Nuclear Power Station and seems to have been used as a landing point for boats for many

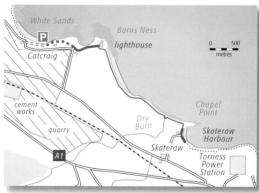

through a gate onto a stony track and follow this by an old limekiln – see **Dunbar to Barns Ness [37]**. Beyond a gate bear left onto a narrow road and follow this down towards Barns Ness Lighthouse, which was one of a chain of lighthouses built to guide ships and boats along this treacherous stretch of coastline into the Firth of Forth. Completed in 1901 by David and Charles Stevenson it was initially lit by a paraffin light before being fully automated in 1986.

Just before the lighthouse turn right onto a path, signposted for the John Muir Way, and follow this along the coast. The path can be a little boggy and wet at times as it proceeds south-east through marram grass where there are great views towards the bigger cliffs of the Scottish Borders coast. It is simple walk, initially alongside a lovely long stony beach, where wading birds search for food.

centuries before a small harbour was built around the early 19th century. It was then used to export limestone from the nearby limekilns and for importing coal, although it was reclaimed by the sea during the late 1800s.

Today Skateraw Bay is a Site of Special Scientific Interest where oystercatcher, curlew, dunlin, skylark, common blue and small copper butterfly, eider ducks and red breasted merganser can be spotted whilst gannets regularly journey from Bass Rock to fish here.

From the little car park at Catcraig beside White Sands, climb a path

Continue to follow the path, with Torness Power Station looming large on the horizon. As Skateraw is approached the path narrows, soon veering right then left to run to the right of a wall and across a footbridge over the Dry Burn. Turn left from the bridge from where the path swings right to continue along the coast, to the left of a fence. Go straight on past a public path for Skateraw Farm then drop down briefly onto a stony beach.

The path is quickly picked up again

START & FINISH: *Catcraig car park (NT709773)*

DISTANCE: *7km; 4.25 miles*

TIME: *2hrs 20mins*

MAP: *OS 67*

TERRAIN: *Tracks & paths*

GRADE: *Easy/Moderate*

Barns Ness Lighthouse from Skateraw

and just before Chapel Point it turns right, hugging the line of the fence. Go around a gate onto a rough road, and follow this around Skateraw Bay, which is a lovely spot to sit and enjoy this quiet corner. Just beyond a small car park a short climb up a path leads to a sumptuous view along the coast to Barns Ness.

From Skateraw Bay retrace your steps along this windswept segment of the East Lothian coastline to Catcraig.

Torness from south of Thorntonloch

Thortonloch is a stunning starting point for a walk. A gorgeous arc of golden sand draws the eye along the coastline to the cliffs of the Scottish Borders. Tranquility reigns as, apart from a couple of houses and a small caravan park, there is nothing but exemplary coastal walking all the way to Dunglass.

Here sits the small but striking Dunglass Collegiate Church – see **Dunglass Mains [40]**. Founded in 1444 by Sir Alexander Home (who for a time was Deputy Sheriff of Berwickshire), it was initially cared for by a college of priests (hence the name collegiate).

During the 16th century south and north transepts and a tower were added but much of the decoration and statues were removed during the Reformation of 1560. Dunglass Church remained in use until the 1700s and remains in remarkably good condition.

From the public car park beside Thorntonloch Caravan Park, turn right, follow the John Muir Way to the right by the entrance of the caravan site (walkers are only allowed through the site if a high tide impedes walking along the beach). Go straight on through a gate, onto Thortonloch Beach, turn right and follow this gorgeous section of sand.

Once past the caravan site bear right, just before the outflow of the Thornton Burn, and follow a path to a bridge. Cross the bridge, turn left and continue along a narrow path by a cottage and over a footbridge. Turn right at a waymark, follow the path as it climbs gradually through a gate then turn left. Follow a magnificent path as it travels south-east high above the coast granting some wonderful views.

In due course the path veers right

START & FINISH: *Thorntonloch car park (NT751745)*

DISTANCE: *7km; 7.25 miles*

TIME: *2hrs 15mins*

MAP: *OS 67*

TERRAIN: *Tracks, paths & beach*

GRADE: *Moderate*

Eventually the path enters a strip of woodland near Bilsdean. Go left at a fork, drop down steps to a junction, turn left and descend past a fantastic waterfall and a burn. The path exits the woodland and crosses a bridge over a burn onto a stony beach. Loose stones are a little awkward to cross over but it is a lovely peaceful spot.

After around 300m bear right from the beach at a waymark from where a path climbs past a path on the right, through scrubby woodland, then above the Dunglass Burn. Keep right at a fork then ahead at a junction to cross an access road onto a path which passes underneath two impressive road bridges to reach a blocked road on the south side of the A1.

Turn left through a railway viaduct, then cross a road to the entrance drive for Dunglass Collegiate Church. Follow this to the church, which is worth spending a little time wandering around, then retrace your steps back to Thortonloch.

above a gorge then left down steps and through a gate from where it prolongs its course above the coast. The waves invariably crash in from the North Sea to the cliffs below, the relentless power evident in an arresting natural arch at the base of the steep embankment.

Looking south-east from Thorntonloch

Dunglass Mains
15th century church & country estate

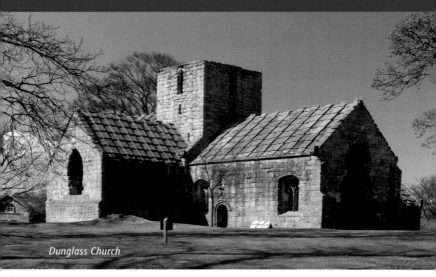

Dunglass Church

Cockburnspath is the start point to this picturesque walk that makes its way to the peaceful surrounds of Dunglass Mains, home to Dunglass Collegiate Church.

The church – see **Thorntonloch to Dunglass [39]** for more info – sits within the manicured grounds and pleasant woodland of Dunglass Estate, which is cut in two by the Dunglass Burn.

The Home family, including Sir Alexander Home, who founded Dunglass Church and was made a Lord of Parliament in 1473, owned the estate during the 14th and early 15th centuries. The Hall family then occupied the estate for 232 years from 1687 to 1919 when the Usher family bought it. They still run the estate today. Robert Burns was particularly taken with Dunglass estate when he

visited in 1787, saying, "Dunglass, the most romantic sweet place I ever saw".

The walk begins from The Square in Cockburnspath, beside the Mercat Cross erected around 1503 to commemorate the marriage of James IV to Margaret Tudor. From here follow The Causeway opposite the cross, past the distinctive red-brick and red-roofed Sparrow Castle, the oldest surviving building in the village. This Grade A-Listed Manor house dates from the 16th century and consists of two houses joined together at right angles.

The Causeway narrows to a track then swings left to run by Cockburnspath Bowling Club. Turn left onto a road, which skirts the eastern edge of the village, and follow the pavement out of Cockburnspath. As the road swings left follow the verge down to a junction near a roundabout

START & FINISH: *The Square, Cockburnspath (NT775711)*

DISTANCE: *4km; 2.5 miles*

TIME: *1hr 20mins*

MAP: *OS 67*

TERRAIN: *Roads, track & paths*

GRADE: *Easy*

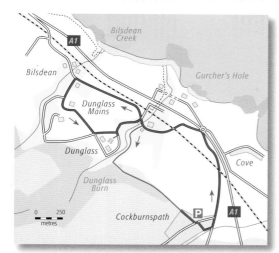

at the A1. Turn left for Oldhamstocks and Dunglass Collegiate Church and walk along this quiet road, passing through a railway arch then crossing Dunglass Bridge.

Pass the entrance drive to Dunglass Church and continue along a roadside verge for 740m, turning left onto a narrow road beside Farm Lodge, signposted for Dunglass Home Farm. Follow this scenic road as it climbs gradually through fine countryside, veering left then right by some cottages to reach a crossroads at Dunglass Mains. Turn left and follow the road to a junction from where the grounds of Dunglass Church can be explored.

To return to Cockburnspath, turn left at the junction and descend through woodland past East Lodge to meet the road. Turn right, re-cross Dunglass Bridge then right again onto a path signposted Cockburnspath Southern Upland Way. After Merse Lodge a track proceeds through Dunglass Dean to reach a path on the left beside a John Muir way sign. Take this path through a gate, follow a field path through another gate from where a path runs to the left of woodland. Beyond another gate continue back into Cockburnspath at Callandar Place. Go straight on by Cockburnspath Primary School and return to Market Square.

Mercat Cross

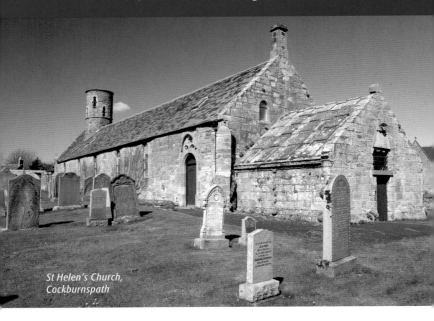

St Helen's Church,
Cockburnspath

The attractive village of Cockburnspath (pronounced Co-burnspath) is, perhaps, best known to walkers as the eastern extremity of the Southern Upland Way. It is also a good base for several short walks that explore the surrounding countryside, including this pleasant ramble that utilises countryside, woodland and coastal paths.

Cockburnspath grew around its market square from the 11th century when it was known as Coldbrandspath. It is thought the name derives from a Dane known as Coldbrand who performed brave deeds and eventually settled here. Cockburnspath developed along what was known as the Great North Road and many armies passed

through the village, especially during the wars between Scotland and England. Oliver Cromwell and his army visited Cockburnspath in 1650 on a campaign that culminated in the Battle of Dunbar. They occupied and destroyed part of Cockburnspath's most impressive building, St Helen's Church, which lies off the south side of The Square. Originally built in the 14th century, the church has a distinctive circular tower at its western gable and a stone-roofed burial vault at its east end. It has been extensively restored, particularly during the 18th century.

From the Mercat Cross walk along Callander Place past Cockburnspath Primary School. Go straight on along a fenced path signposted Dunbar John

START & FINISH: *The Square, Cockburnspath (NT775711)*
DISTANCE: *5km; 3 miles*
TIME: *1hr 30mins*
MAP: *OS 67*
TERRAIN: *Roads, track & paths*
GRADE: *Easy/Moderate*

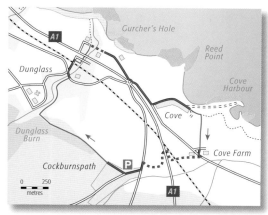

a railway bridge. Take a right onto the John Muir Way, which descends through woodland to pass under two road bridges to reach the 17th century Old Dunglass Bridge. Leave the John Muir Way by turning right over the bridge and follow a gorse-lined track onto a minor road, which leads past some houses to a roundabout at the A1.

Go left here onto a side road signposted to Cove, then the next left where a narrow road sweeps right into the historic coastal village of Cove described in more detail in **Cove & Pease Bay** [42], to reach a car park. Overlooking the sea is a lovely little bronze sculpture commemorating the Eyemouth disaster, described in the walk around **Eyemouth Harbour** [50}.

Muir Way. This path skirts woodland to the left with good views across farmland and along the coast to Barns Ness Lighthouse.

Once through a gate continue along the path, exiting the woodland by a gate from where a field path reaches Dunglass Dean. Go through a gate then turn right at a John Muir Way sign and follow this woodland track to a road.

Turn left over Dunglass Bridge then immediately right opposite the road to Dunglass Collegiate Church and under

Keep right past the houses, the track on the left descends to Cove Harbour, to a signpost and bear right at a fork and go through a gate. Just before the next gate bear left, follow a path to a fork and go right, through a gate for Cockburnspath.

A field path heads inland, crossing straight over a rough access road to Cove Farm, from where a track drops down to a main road. Go left then right and follow a track past some cottages and under the railway. The track turns right to pass under the A1 and continues back to Cockburnspath. Turn left then right onto Hoprig Road and back to The Square.

Eyemouth Disaster sculpture by Jill Watson

42

Cove & Pease Bay

Picturesque harbour & impressive cliffs

Cove Harbour

ove's red sandstone cliffs form a natural harbour which has been utilised by local fishermen since the 1600s. By 1831 a village and harbour had been built by local landowners, the Halls of Dunglass, to house the estate's 20 fishing and farm working families.

The population declined during the 1920s but the harbour, pier, breakwater and cottages that remain are all listed structures of architectural and historical interest. The coastline here is also famed for its outstanding geology, which includes carboniferous strata, fossil fauna, fossil spores and tropical plants.

Take a right from the car park at Cove, follow the road a short distance then bear right at a fork through a gate. Go left at the next two gates and follow a path, which runs high above the shore, granting magnificent views of Cove Harbour and the remarkable geological formations, with steep slopes dropping left to the ragged coastline.

Once above the gorgeous, sandy Pease Bay the path descends steps and crosses a bridge over a burn. Go through a gap in a wall then a gate onto a minor road at Old Linhead. Turn left and descend to the entrance of Pease Bay Leisure Park. Turn right here through a gate onto the Southern Upland Way, signposted to Abbey St Bathans.

Pass through the next gate into the Wildlife Reserve of **Pease Dean [43]** and follow the path through Scots Pine woodland to a footbridge on the left. Take this over the Pease Burn then a right, from where a path soon climbs steeps steps to a junction. Turn left for Pease Bridge.

The path now rises gradually through mixed woodland, where the distinct smell of ramsons linger during the spring, as do colourful bluebells, red campion and primrose. Once through a gate the path exits Pease Dean at the

START & FINISH: *Cove village car park (NT780718)*

DISTANCE: *8km; 5 miles*

TIME: *2hrs 40mins*

MAP: *OS 67*

TERRAIN: *Roads, tracks & paths*

GRADE: *Moderate*

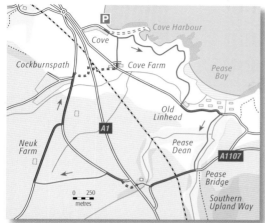

At a road, turn left and climb gradually for 200m to a way-marked track on the left. Follow this then turn next right onto an old Right of Way.

Bounded by hedgerows the track crosses farmland through two gates to gain a minor road. Take a right, walk past Neuk Farm then turn left at a T-junction and descend a roadside verge into Cockburnspath.

Once past the war memorial turn right, back onto the signposted Southern Upland Way. Follow a track underneath the A1 then a railway line to a row of cottages and a road. Turn left then right onto another track and cross a rough access road to Cove Farm, from where a field path heads towards the sea. Descend through a gate and turn left turn back to Cove.

A1107 beside Pease Bridge.

Turn right, follow the roadside verge over the railway line. After 250m bear right into woodland where a waymarked path crosses an old stone bridge then a stile beside the ruin of Cockburnspath Tower, which dates from the early 16th century. Turn left, climb a path over another stile then follow a track under the A1 road bridge.

Pease Bay

43

Pease Dean

A wooded gorge, teeming with wildlife

Pease Dean

Scottish Wildlife Trust's Pease Dean reserve provides simple, pleasant and peaceful walking where a wonderful variety of flora and fauna can be enjoyed.

Pease Dean is one of the few pockets of woodland along the Berwickshire Coast where a mixture of native and non-native species of tree exist. The likes of sessile oak, Scots pine, ash, hazel and alder line the steep banks that surround the Pease Burn and the Tower Burn and provide shelter for a magnificent array of wildflowers, including primrose, wood sorrel, wood anemone, buttercup, ramsons, bluebell and ferns.

The woodland and riverbanks are a haven for northern brown argus, small blue and small heath butterflies, as well as dipper, kingfisher and marsh tit, whilst the wet and sheltered character of the riverbanks support a variety of

mosses and liverworts, usually found much further west.

The walk also climbs to the 39.6m (130ft) high red sandstone Pease Bridge which when opened in 1786, was the tallest bridge in the world. The bridge carries the A1107, the former

START & FINISH: *Pease Bay Leisure Park car park (NT794707)*
DISTANCE: *3km; 1.75 miles*
TIME: *45mins*

MAP: *OS 67*
TERRAIN: *Tracks & paths*
GRADE: *Easy*

Edinburgh to Berwick turnpike road over the deep gorge of Pease Burn, an otherwise formidble barrier to travellers. Designed by David Henderson, the bridge was admired by Scotland's most famous bridge builder Thomas Telford and appears in Turner's sketch books from 1801 and 1818.

Start from Pease Bay Leisure Park, where visitors are allowed to leave their vehicles in a small car park at the entrance. Turn left out of the car park and cross the Pease Burn via a footbridge. Once over, turn right around a barrier and walk through the caravan site, passing through a gate into Pease Dean reserve. Follow the track for about 30m then turn left onto a path, which soon begins to climb quite steeply through woodland. After a steep flight of steps the gradient eases, with the path continuing simply up a few more flight of steps, to exit Pease Dean onto the A1107.

Turn right, cross over Pease Bridge then make a right through a gate back

into Pease Dean. Descend the path, lined with wildflowers during spring and summer, with steep drops down to the right into the gorge below. In due course the path sweeps left to a fork.

Keep straight on, taking the left fork signposted for Tower Dean. Follow the path through the woodland, crossing a boardwalk over a boggier section of ground. Ascend then descend some steps then cross a footbridge. After descending more steps the path splits. Go right down steps and once over a footbridge the path turns left and hugs the right bank of a burn.

In due course the path veers right and ascends gradually to a point high above the Tower Burn, then descends steps to reach the banks of the Pease Burn. Turn left, follow the path along the riverbank, keeping straight on by a footbridge on the right.

The path then ascends through lovely Scots pine woodland before dropping down steps and through a gate. Beyond the next gate, cross the road back into Pease Dean Leisure Park.

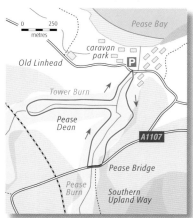

44

Siccar Point
James Hutton & the Scottish Enlightenment

St Helen's Church

he importance of the geology between Pease Bay and Siccar Point cannot be underestimated. In 1788 the renowned Scottish geologist James Hutton made a boat trip, with his friends James Hall and John Playfair, from Dunglass Burn to Siccar Point. Hutton, who was born nearby at Reston in 1726, was already convinced that the age of the earth was far older than the considered creation date of 4004BC but he needed more evidence.

He discovered this at Siccar Point. Here Hutton found beds of grey sedimentary rock which had been deposited as horizontal layers, but then turned vertical by movements in the earth's crust and eroded. On top of these rocks, new horizontal layers of red sand and gravel had been deposited. It was clear to Hutton that for all these processes to have happened, the time difference between the two deposits had to be millions of

years, not a mere 4,000. Today, we know it was about 55 million.

Upon reaching the cliffs above Siccar Point today the proof that Hutton sought is clearly visible as are the extraordinary geological formations along much of the coastline, that form the basis of this fine walk.

From Pease Bay Leisure Park, where visitors are allowed to leave their vehicles in a small car park just at the entrance, turn left onto a road and cross the Pease Burn by a footbridge. Continue along the road as it climbs steeply by the caravan site then go through a gate on the left signposted for Siccar Point. Follow a path to the left of the road up steps, which climb steeply onto a cliff top path where there are amazing views over Pease Bay all the way to Fife.

Go through a gate and keep along the path as it swings right above Greenheugh Point and heads east, high above the coast with the geology

START & FINISH: *Pease Bay Leisure Park car park (NT794707)*

DISTANCE: *5.5km; 3.5 miles*

TIME: *1hr 50mins*

MAP: *OS 67*

TERRAIN: *Roads, tracks & paths*

GRADE: *Easy/Moderate*

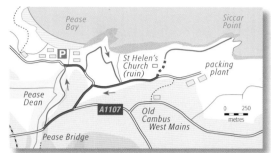

Point – a steep path descends to the point but it is recommended that the view be enjoyed from the information board.

Retrace your steps, enjoying magnificent views towards Bass Rock, back to the Siccar Point car park. Turn right, walk along the road passing the outward-bound path to gain the A1107. Turn right, follow the roadside verge for 250m and just before Pease Bridge turn sharp right into Pease Dean where a grassy path heads into woodland. The path descends gently down several flights of steps then more steeply to a junction near the Pease Burn. Turn right, follow the track through a gate out of Pease Dean. Walk through Pease Bay Leisure Park, exiting round a barrier, then left across the footbridge over the Pease Burn, back to the start.

below very apparent. The path soon heads inland passing through three gates to reach a minor road.

Walk left along the road for 500m and just before Siccar Point visitor car park bear left to a track and over a stile. From here a grassy field track passes the ruin of the 12th century St Helen's Church. This served the parish of Aldcambus until united with the parish of Cockburnspath after the Reformation of 1560, see **Cockburnspath to Cove** [41].

At a wall turn right and follow the field edge to the headland above Siccar

Siccar Point - grey vertical beds (right), overlain by red horizontal beds (left)

45

Fast Castle

Ruins that inspired great writers & painters

Fast Castle ruins

ast Castle stands, somewhat precariously, on a rocky headland projecting into the North Sea north-west of St Abb's Head and is the dramatic objective of this short walk from Dowlaw Farm.

Although very little remains of the castle, its history is long and fascinating. There are no records as to when it was first built, but it certainly predates 1346, when it was occupied by English troops following the Battle of Neville's Cross, near Durham. In 1410 Patrick Dunbar captured the castle although it later passed into the hands of his great rivals, the Home family. Margaret Tudor stayed overnight in 1503, as did Mary, Queen of Scots in 1566, although by this time it had been destroyed, rebuilt

and captured by the English in 1547 during Henry VIII's 'Rough Wooing' of Scotland. By 1609 it lay in ruin.

Although this is a short walk, the route back to Dowlaw is uphill all the way and great care is required if exploring the castle ruins. The drawbridge which once linked Fast Castle's rocky headland to the mainland has been replaced by an exposed concrete footbridge with handrails and the headland is surrounded by steep cliffs. This is not a spot for small children. Not much survives save for part of the wall forming the north-east corner and associated sections of tumbled masonry.

Despite this, it is an impressive and atmospheric location. Sir Walter Scott

START & FINISH: *Dowlaw Farm car park (NT856702)*

DISTANCE: *2.5km; 1.5 miles*

TIME: *45 mins*

MAP: *OS 67*

TERRAIN: *Paths*

GRADE: *Moderate. Crossing to the castle ruins is exposed*

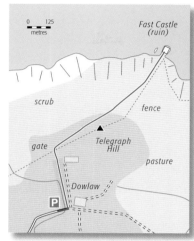

along heathery slopes where steepish drops slope left down to the shore. When the path forks go left where it begins to steepen, and the first view of Fast Castle's dramatic aspect comes into view. A flight of steps descend a steep incline from where the path runs to the left of a fence then above a steep gorge. A grassy path now descends steadily to cross over the concrete bridge to the castle ruins.

It is a spectacular spot with sea pinks and campion clinging to the cliffs that are home to several small colonies of guillemots, kittiwakes and shags – the cliffs and rocks are splattered with guano.

As with the majority of the Scottish Borders coastline the geology is very impressive as are the views of the spiky Wheat Stack and Little Rooks.

Retrace the outward route to Dowlaw, taking into account the steep ascent of around 300 feet, giving legs and lungs a good workout.

used Fast Castle as the inspiration for Wolf's Craig in his 1819 novel *The Bride of Lammermoor* and the ruins were a favourite location of the great British watercolourist J.M.W.Turner, who sketched them from land and sea, in 1801, 1818, 1822 and 1831.

Dowlaw is signposted from the A1107, accessed from the A1 south of Cockburnspath, and has a car park at the end of the three kilometre access road. From the car park turn left just before the farm, cross a stile beside a gate and descend a path through a strip of woodland to a gate, just to the left of a row of cottages. Go over a stile here, cross a field path and pass through a gate, beyond which there is an incredible view along the coast to Bass Rock and the Lomond Hills.

Take the right branch of a fork onto a well-worn field path, which heads north-east, contouring the slopes of Telegraph Hill. A stony path continues

46

Coldingham Loch
Farmland, lochs & cliff-tops

Descending to St Abb's Head

This lovely walk passes through a fantastic diversity of landscape, where rolling views of Scottish Borders countryside are replaced by the gorgeous, tranquil surrounds of Coldingham Loch, which in turn leads to one of the finest stretches of coastline in Scotland.

Start from Coldingham Luckenbooth, home to the local post office, tourist information, a coffee shop and the superb Coldingham Priory Interpretation Centre. Luckenbooths (or Locked Booths) were merchant stalls found in Edinburgh during the Middle Ages and the city's first permanent shops. Coldingham Luckenbooth was a community led project that opened after Coldingham Post Office closed in 2009.

Cross Bridge Street onto School Road, walk past the Mercat Cross, which dates from 1815 and after Coldingham Primary School turn right onto West Loch Road. Beyond several houses this single-track road climbs steadily through rolling countryside with fine views south to the distant Cheviot Hills.

After approximately 2km pass the entrance of Westloch Farm and farm barns then, after another 200 metres but before the entrance road to Coldingham Loch and West Loch House Estate, turn right over a stile signposted 'Footpath'. There is no path to speak of, so follow the left edge of a field beside woodland and cross over three more stiles to a rough track close to Coldingham Loch.

The loch is one of Scotland's oldest fisheries and a Site of Special Scientific Interest, primarily because of it being a nutrient rich loch. Wildlife here includes long-tailed duck, whooper swan, widgeon, pink-footed and greylag geese. It is a beautiful, tranquil spot.

Walk rightwards along the rough track to beyond a gate where it joins a track coming from the farm barns, heading north-east around the southern end of the loch. After the next gate the track veers left again to cross open farmland where the remains of iron-age settlements stand. At the head of Coldingham Loch the track reaches a

START & FINISH: *Coldingham Luckenbooth (NT904659)*
DISTANCE: *11.5km; 7 miles*
TIME: *3hrs 45mins*

MAP: *OS 67*
TERRAIN: *Roads, tracks & paths*
GRADE: *Easy/Moderate*

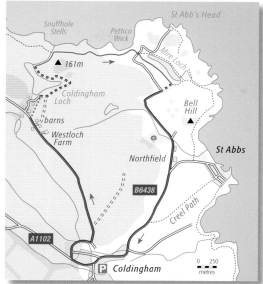

steadily, turning right over a stile then left after a few metres over another. Follow a field's left edge (where livestock graze) as it sweeps right, eventually passing through a gate to gain the St Abb's Head access road.

Go straight on through another gate, follow a path over a stile and along the wooded southern shore of Mire Loch. At its head make a right and climb a steep, rough track. At the top bear left onto a minor road, which meanders through lovely countryside, passing through a gate beside a cattle grid.

In due course drop down through a gate, walk past several cottages and St Abb's Visitor Centre at Northfield. Go straight ahead onto the B6438 initially following the roadside verge, but after the Creel Path – see **St Abbs & Coldingham [48]** – along the pavement back to Coldingham.

gate. Don't go through this; instead turn right, cross the field, with the fence to the left, past a stile. Cross the next stile onto the coast path and turn right where a steep climb reaches a viewpoint, and a stunning view along the spectacular Scottish Borders coastline and St Abb's Head.

Once through a gate the path drops

Coldingham Loch

47

St Abb's Head

A spectacular headland of seabirds & steep cliffs

St Abb's Head Lighthouse

The scenery, wildlife and geology in and around St Abb's Head is quite breathtaking and a selection of excellent paths make this route an absolute joy. The headland is a National Nature Reserve, under the care of the National Trust for Scotland. Throughout the year the cliffs are home to an enormous bird colony including nearly 40,000 guillemots, kittiwakes and razorbills, plus shags, fulmars, herring gulls and puffins. Furthermore, the crystal clear waters below form part of Scotland's only Voluntary Marine Reserve, which protects the diverse natural environment as well as serving the needs of fishermen, divers, surfers and sailors. The walk also follows the shores of Mire Loch, where the waters, reedbeds

and woodland provide a great habitat for migrating birds, mute swans, frogs, toads, butterflies and damselflies.

From the St Abb's Visitor Centre pay & display car park at Northfield, take the path, which runs by the visitor centre then alongside the B6438. It turns left at a pocket of woodland and once through a gate begins a gradual ascent up and over the cliffs where a series of twisted, rocky chimneys, ledges and sea-stacks, plunging vertically into the North Sea's crystal clear waters, are incredibly impressive. Parts of the cliffs are covered in guano giving an idea of the resident birdlife.

Keep to the cliff path as it descends quite steeply by the gorgeous Burnmouth Harbour and Horsecastle Bay. Once through a gate the path

START & FINISH: *St Abb's visitor centre car park (NT913674)*
DISTANCE: *6km; 3.75 miles*
TIME: *2hrs*

MAP: *OS 67*
TERRAIN: *Roads, tracks & paths*
GRADE: *Moderate*

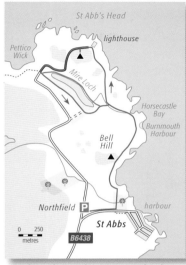

lighthouse, before following the access road as it meanders downhill to Pettico Wick, where 400 million years old sedimentary rocks are clearly visible.

Just before a cattle grid, turn left onto a grassy path, which immediately splits, offering a route along either shore of Mire Loch. For the northern shore go left and follow a grassy lochside path. At its head, just before a stile, bear left down steps to a junction then turn left. For the southern shore, take the right path over a stile and climb above the loch by reedbeds and through woodland to a rough track heading up right to the lighthouse access road.

Turn left and descend through a gate to meet the northern shore route and continue for 50m to the outward-bound path near Horsecastle Bay. Turn right and retrace your steps back to the start.

travels underneath a steep embankment, home to wild thyme and rock rose, a vital food source for the nationally rare northern brown argus butterfly, which can be seen here between June and July.

A steady pull, bounded on either side by steep embankments, then ensues. Keep left as a path comes in from the right and continue to reach St Abb's Head Lighthouse, a wonderfully wild and windswept spot. Built in 1862 by David and Thomas Stevenson, the lighthouse was originally powered by coal and oil and manned by three full-time keepers until it was automated in 1994. Walk to the left of the lighthouse and surrounding buildings to an access road from where there is an incredible view west along the Scottish Borders coastline. It is worth ascending to the summit of the small hill south of the

South to St Abbs

St Abbs to Berwick-upon-Tweed

Beach huts at Coldingham Bay

he superb Berwickshire Coastal Path runs the entire length of this coastline, crossing the border into England to conclude at the historic and popular town of Berwick-upon-Tweed. En route, quiet country roads, farm tracks, lochs, woodland, countryside paths and ancient paths link towns and villages such as St Abbs, Coldingham and Eyemouth with the coastline underpinning the fantastic walking and exemplary scenery along the Scottish Borders coastline [48].

St Abbs & Coldingham [48] are linked by the ancient Creel Path with Coldingham home to the impressive Coldingham Priory and the gorgeous Coldingham Sands. The Creel Path is also utilised on the route from St Abbs to Eyemouth [49] with a return to Coldingham along a section of the Æbbe Way.

The route round Eyemouth Town [50] takes in a large section of the coast as well as visiting Gunsgreen House and the Eyemouth Museum for an insight into the town's history of fishing and smuggling.

Leaving the Scottish Borders behind, the remaining three walks centre on the Northumbrian town of Berwick-upon-Tweed. With its broad selection of accommodation, shops, pubs and restaurants, and excellent transport infrastructure, Berwick provides a wonderful base to explore the historic town and surrounding countryside.

Fought over for centuries by the Scots and English, the paved paths of Berwick-upon-Tweed's fortified town walls are easily linked with coastal paths for the route to **Fisherman's Haven** [51], a lovely beach on the outskirts of the town.

As well as the town walls, **Berwick's Bridges** [52] are conspicuous landmarks; this triumvirate with their striking architecture spans the River Tweed. The oldest structure is Berwick Bridge, which dates from the 17th century while the Royal Tweed Road Bridge is the newest having been opened in 1928. The finest of the three is the magnificent Royal Border Bridge, and a lovely walk around Berwick-upon-Tweed visits all of the bridges.

The final walk celebrates the association between **Berwick & LS Lowry** [53], the distinguished artist, renowned for his depictions of the English industrial north-west, but also for the series of paintings, drawings and sketches of Berwick and its people

Berwick-upon-Tweed town walls

48 St Abbs & Coldingham

Coldingham Priory & the Creel Path

Coldingham Sands

The villages of St Abbs and Coldingham are linked by the Creel Path, a route that has been in use for more than 1,000 years. Before a village was established at St Abbs, Coldingham was the main settlement and the fishermen carried their gear along the Creel Path down to Coldingham Shore (now St Abbs), from where they would return later in the day with creels of fish. Today the path provides a simple and scenic start to a walk that visits the impressive setting of Coldingham Priory and the beautiful Coldingham Sands.

In its heyday Coldingham Priory was one of Scotland's most important religious buildings. Its history extends back to 1098, when King Edgar permitted monks from Durham to erect a priory church here. It soon grew to become the second wealthiest monastery in Scotland, second only to Edinburgh's Holyrood Abbey. At its most powerful, 30 monks and 70 staff ran Coldingham

Priory with income from farm rents, wool, grain, timber, livestock and fishing.

However with power came enemies and Coldingham Priory was attacked several times over the centuries with its end coming in 1648 when a group of Royalist sympathizers took shelter in the church with their store of gunpowder. Oliver Cromwell and his army besieged the site and it was largely destroyed. Thankfully it has been restored, with much of the repair taking place in the 19th century.

From St Abbs Harbour exit left onto a narrow road then bear right and follow a path up to Seaview Terrace. Go straight on onto Creel Road and at a gate bear right onto the Creel Path. Follow this historic route as it heads inland through lovely countryside.

The path drops gradually then climbs through a tunnel of Hawthorn Trees, which have been shaped and bent by the wind. At the B6438 turn left and drop down into the attractive, sleepy

START & FINISH: St Abbs Harbour (NT920673)

DISTANCE: 5km; 3 miles

TIME: 1hr 30mins

MAP: OS 67

TERRAIN: Roads, tracks & paths

GRADE: Easy

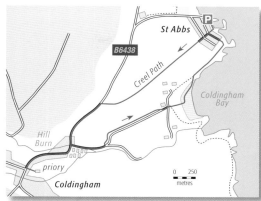

Priory. Within the graveyard is Collector's Corner, an unusual collection of gravestone's and masonry that were carved during the 19th century.

Exit the grounds right back onto Main Street and retrace your steps over the bridge crossing Hill Burn. Immediately turn right for Coldingham Bay and follow a quiet country

village of Coldingham, which grew in the 1100s alongside the priory.

Once across a bridge over Hill Burn walk through the village along Fisher's Brae (previously called Cadger's Brae as it allowed access to Coldingham Shore where the cadger's, or fish merchants, bought fish) then Main Street, to a junction and a small car park. Go though this to reach the striking red façade of Coldingham

road by a caravan site. Once past the site bear left onto a path, which runs parallel with the road. After a car park and hotel a tarmac path descends to the gorgeous arc of Coldingham Bay.

Turn left, walk along the beach and at its far end, climb steep steps onto a path. Turn right and follow this into St Abbs. At a fork go left onto Murrayfield, then turn right onto Seaview Terrace and descend back to the harbour.

Coldingham Priory

A rugged section of coastline

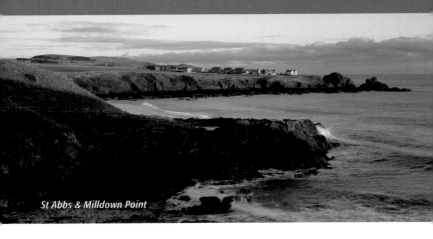

St Abbs & Milldown Point

St Abbs only developed as a village in 1833 but by the mid-19th century it had become a busy fishing port (it still has a working harbour). At the end of the 19th century the local laird renamed the village St Abbs after St Æbbe, a Northumbrian princes, who founded a monastery near St Abb's Head in 635AD. Today a variety of outdoor pursuits, including scuba diving and walking, continue to draw visitors. St Abbs provides a picturesque start point to this walk while Eyemouth has lots of shops, pubs and cafes to relax and refuel before returning to St Abbs via Coldingham along the Æbbe Way.

From St Abbs Harbour exit left onto a narrow road then bear right and follow a path up to Seaview Terrace. Turn left onto Murrayfield, follow this to its end then turn right onto the Berwickshire Coastal Path. At steps drop left down onto Coldingham Sands. Walk across the beach, bearing left onto a path just before a steep embankment.

Walk around Milldown Point, go left down steps then across a bridge over Milldown Burn. After a stony beach, steps climb high above the coast with the path eventually descending to Linkim Shore. A grassy path travels along the top of the beach, passing a path signed 'Coldingham via Fleurs Farm'. Keep straight on and climb in-between steep embankments, cross two footbridges then ascend a flight of steps. Turn left and follow field-edge paths for approximately 1.25km above a rugged stretch of coast to Killiedraught Bay, on the outskirts of Eyemouth. The path sweeps left then right alongside a caravan site. At the site's end fork left down onto a beach. Cross this then turn left onto Marine Parade and walk into Eyemouth – see **Eyemouth Harbour [50]**.

Retrace your steps back to Linkim Shore and turn left for Fleurs Farm. The Æbbe Walk climbs up a slope and crosses two stiles. A narrow field-edge path runs inland to the right of a fence

START & FINISH: *St Abbs Harbour (NT920673)*

DISTANCE: *14km; 8.5 miles*

TIME: *4hrs 30mins*

MAP: *OS 67*

TERRAIN: *Roads, tracks & paths*

GRADE: *Moderate/Strenuous*

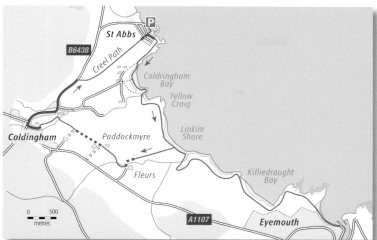

to Fleurs Farm. Just before various farm buildings turn right through a gate onto a woodland path. Once over a footbridge and stile, a field path proceeds through two gates to Paddockmyre. Go straight on at a crossroads from where a farm track crosses a field's left edge. As the track swings left for Coldinghamlaw go straight on through a gate onto a field-edge path.

Once through another gate and over a footbridge, fork right, cross another bridge then turn left over a stile.

Beyond two gates a woodland path culminates at a track. Turn left then right onto The Bow, which continues into Coldingham.

Leave the Æbbe Way by turning right onto Bridge Street then right again onto Main Street (B6438). Follow the pavement out of Coldingham for just over 1km then turn right onto the Creel Path between **St Abbs & Coldringham** [48], which makes its way back into St Abbs at Seaview Terrace. Continue straight on back to the harbour.

Killkiedraught Bay

50

Eyemouth Town
Exploring the historic town & harbour

Eyemouth Harbour

*E*yemouth is an attractive town, which sits at the mouth of the Eye Water. Fishing has been vital to Eyemouth's economy since 1298 but it also led to the tragedy with which the town is inextricably linked. On October 14th 1881 a vicious storm whipped up and, due to the limitations of Eyemouth harbour's entrance, the fishing fleet already out at sea could not re-enter. 189 fishermen, including 129 from Eyemouth, lost their lives that day, leaving the town in despair. The story of the disaster is detailed in the excellent Eyemouth Museum on Manse Road, open Tuesday-Sunday between April and October.

Situated beside the harbour is the striking Gunsgreen House. Built by John Adam, its merchant owners, John and David Nisbet, used the house for nefarious smuggling activities. The cellars and roofspace were specially adapted to allow highly profitable products such as brandy, tobacco and tea to be secretly delivered. Ultimately Gunsgreen House fell into disrepair but was restored in the 1990s by the Gunsgreen House Trust and is open to the public between March and October from Thursday- Monday.

From Harbour Road follow the quayside by Manse Road, then turn left over the Eye Water via a bridge. Turn left along the harbour's eastern side. Once over another bridge walk by the RNLI station and Gunsgreen House – a little to the right stands Nisbet's Tower, which used to be a dovecot for Gunsgreen.

Once past a fishmarket climb a path up a grassy embankment crossing a narrow road. Turn right and follow a path through a gate to gain a coastal

START & FINISH: *Eyemouth Harbour (NT946644)*

DISTANCE: *7.5km; 4.5 miles*

TIME: *2hrs 15mins*

MAP: *OS 67*

TERRAIN: *Roads, tracks & paths*

GRADE: *Easy/Moderate*

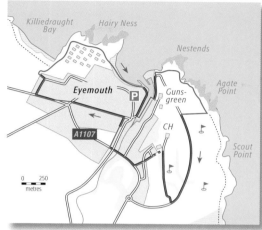

Eyemouth Cemetery. At Northburn Road go straight across and follow a parkland path back to the A1107.

At Hinkar Way turn right. Walk along the pavement but as it swings right, turn left then go straight onto a path, which swings right and heads towards the coast. Keep right at the next junction then swing left to the Berwickshire Coastal Path. Go straight on, where the path descends by Killiedraught Bay, swinging right to run alongside a caravan site. At the site's end fork left down onto a beach. Cross this then turn left and follow Marine Parade back to the harbour.

path. Take the right path at a fork and once through another gate, the path skirts the perimeter of Eyemouth Golf Course. At a fork go left where the path sweeps right to a wall. Turn left, then at a signpost for Eyemouth go right through a gate. Carefully follow a path across the golf course, exiting left onto a pavement.

Walk south for 1km then turn right onto the entrance road for Eyemouth Golf Course. Follow this to a lane on the left called Stebbing's Rise sign-posted 'Eyemouth Town Centre'. Descend over two side roads onto Gunsgreen Park, then turn right onto the A1107.

Follow the pavement, which crosses the Eye Water, over Victoria Road onto a path, which turns right. Continue through woodland and parkland onto a lane, which culminates at Coldingham Road. Go left and keep on past Eyemouth Primary School then

Gunsgreen House

51

Fisherman's Haven
Through the town to a sandy beach

Berwick-upon-Tweed

The fascinating history of Berwick-upon-Tweed is confusing to say the least. From the late 11th century the town, and its port, was one of the most important in Scotland and this continued until Edward I of England sacked Berwick in 1296, killing 8,000 residents in the process. Consequently over the course of the next 200 years Berwick changed hands between Scotland and England no fewer than 14 times and has remained English since 1482 (however, just to add to the confusion the local football team, Berwick Rangers play in the Scottish League).

The famous town walls were erected during the 14th century when Edward I fortified the town against Scottish attack and today they are a legacy of Berwick's history and can be walked, providing tangible evidence of the battles fought over the centuries to gain control of the town.

The striking Town Hall on Marygate dates from 1754 and marks the starting point for this walk round the coast to the cove of Fisherman's Haven, then back beside the town walls. With the Town Hall at your back turn left and follow Marygate onto Woolmarket and continue to Ravensdowne. Go straight on up a flight of steps onto the Town Walls and walk along a narrow lane, passing the impressive Lions House, to a junction. Here there are fine views of the Northumberland Coast. Go right and then left down a flight of steps and through an archway under the walls.

At a fork, go right and follow the path away from the Town Walls sweeping left to a flight of steps beside a row of houses. Turn right, descend the steps onto Pier Road, turn left and walk along the coast. Just before the harbour bear left onto a single-track road, passing several houses and a car park. Follow

START & FINISH: *Town Hall, Marygate (NT999529)*

DISTANCE: *4.5km; 2.75miles*

TIME: *1hr 30mins*

MAP: *OS 75*

TERRAIN: *Roads, paths & beach*

GRADE: *Easy*

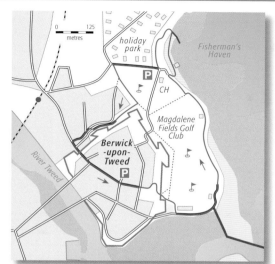

course path. Turn right, follow the path towards the golf course clubhouse and once above Fisherman's Haven, turn right and descend a flight of steps to this sandy cove. It is a lovely spot for a break. Turn left, cross the beach, to an old harbour wall and climb a steep flight of steps to reach a holiday park. Turn left and follow a path to a car park. Walk to the right along the holiday park access road to a junction and turn left onto a tarmac path to

the road and as it sweeps left to another car park, go straight on to gain the Berwickshire Coastal Path.

This grassy path runs above the North Sea, to the right of Magdalene Fields Golf Course, with great views along the Berwickshire Coast. The path soon passes by a coastguard watch-tower and then reaches a tarmac golf

the right of the golf course. At a fork bear left and just before the town walls turn right onto a path, which runs to the right of the walls. Pass some cottages and a car park onto Well Close Square and continue along Scott's Place to Castlegate. Turn left, pass underneath Scots Gate onto Marygate and the Town Hall.

Fisherman's Haven

52

Berwick's Bridges
Road & rail across the River Tweed

Berwick Town Walls & Barracks

Berwick-upon-Tweed is dominated by the three distinctive bridges, which span the River Tweed near its outflow with the North Sea. The newest of the bridges is the Royal Tweed Bridge, which was opened in 1928 to divert traffic from the adjacent Berwick Bridge, and used to be part of the old A1 between Edinburgh and London.

The fine red sandstone Berwick Bridge dates from the 17th century and is actually the fifth bridge to be erected on that site (the first was built in 1199). Work started on the Berwick Bridge in 1611 after James VI of Scotland had criticised the state of the wooden bridge here when he crossed into England in 1603 to claim the English throne. Berwick Bridge was eventually opened in 1624.

However it is the spectacular Royal Border Bridge, which is the finest of the three. This wonderful viaduct was the final link of the Newcastle to Berwick railway line and was opened in 1850 by Queen Victoria having been designed by the English civil engineer Robert Stephenson.

With the Town Hall on Marygate at your back walk through the town centre past two mini-roundabouts. Just before the Elizabethan Scot Gate archway, turn left and climb Bankhill. At the top take a sharp right through a gate onto the town walls. Climb a flight of steps on the left to a viewpoint, which was the site of Megs Mount, a platform of heavy guns used to protect the town.

Drop back down to the town walls, turn left and cross Scots Gate (in the 16th century this was the border of the town), from where the path continues by Cumberland Bastion to reach the Brass Bastion. Bear right here and walk south along the top of the wall past the

START & FINISH: *Town Hall, Marygate (NT999529)*
DISTANCE: *4.5km; 2.75miles*
TIME: *1hr 30mins*

MAP: *OS 75*
TERRAIN: *Roads & paths*
GRADE: *Easy*

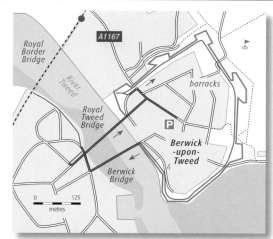

follow this across the River Tweed. At the end, turn right onto West End, pass under the Royal Tweed Bridge and then bear right onto a riverside path, which runs adjacent to Riverside Road. Follow the path beside the Tweed to reach the amazing Royal Border Bridge, which is more than 600m (2,000ft) in length and carries the railway 38m (125ft) above the river. Retrace your steps along the riverside path and just as the Royal Tweed Bridge is approached turn right and ascend a flight of steps to reach the A1167 (the old A1). Turn left and re-cross the River Tweed by the Royal Tweed Bridge, which provides a fantastic view of both the Royal Border and Berwick bridges. Once across continue onto Golden Square, turn right onto Marygate and return to the Town Hall.

striking Berwick Barracks (these were once the oldest barracks in Britain and are now a museum) and an old gunpowder building.

The path drops down through a gate and then by Fisher's Fort, where there are good views of the North Sea. It then sweeps right by Coxon's Tower (also known as the Bulwark in the Sands) to arrive at Bridge End. Go left onto the striking Berwick Bridge and

Berwick Bridge

The Lions

The artist Laurence Stephen Lowry is renowned for his depictions of the English industrial north-west, where he lived and worked. However his paintings of Berwick have become equally celebrated. He visited the town on a number of occasions from the 1930s until his death in 1976 and painted Berwick and its people many times. He was particularly drawn to Berwick Town Hall and the walls that encircled the town. This walk travels around Berwick and out to Spittal, on the River Tweed's south bank, visiting a number of places that Lowry painted and was inspired by.

With the Town Hall on Marygate at your back, walk a short distance up through the town, turn left onto West Street, left onto Easter Wynd and then right onto Eastern Lane. Shortly after, turn left through an archway and follow Shoe Lane onto Bridge Street. Cross straight over onto Sally Port (Lowry loved Berwick's narrow closes); follow this under the town walls to Quay Walls. Turn left then left again through an archway onto Sandgate and go right onto Palace Street.

Upon reaching the 18th century guardhouse where Palace Street swings left, turn right then left to gain the town walls and follow them round past Fisher's Fort. Just before a gate turn left down steps and then right through an archway onto Pier Road – Lowry sketched the harbour view in 1956. Follow Pier Road but before the harbour bear left and walk along a road to a car park. Here sits a shelter, which Lowry painted as *On the Sands* in 1959. The road climbs by the car park then veers left through another car park. A path skirts Berwick Cricket Club's left edge and continues by a row of houses. At a fork go left to an

START & FINISH: *Town Hall, Marygate (NT999529)*
DISTANCE: *10.5km; 6.5 miles*
TIME: *3hrs 30mins*
MAP: *OS 75*
TERRAIN: *Roads, paths & beach*
GRADE: *Easy/Moderate*

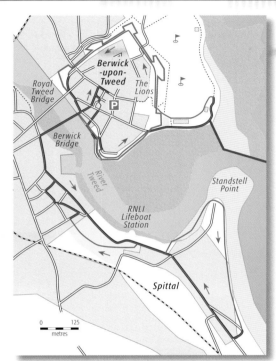

the Royal Tweed Bridge to Bridge Terrace and Berwick Bridge. Cross the bridge over the Tweed, bear left onto Main Street then left onto Dock Road, where Lowry spent time painting.

Follow Dock Road for approximately 1km. Once past the Lifeboat Station and a fenced area, turn left, walk along a beach around Sandstell Point, turn right through a car park and follow a path onto Spittal Promenade. Spittal developed as a Victorian spa town and famous Lowry works like *Man Looking Out to Sea* were painted here.

Turn right onto South Greenwich Road, then right onto Main Street, which is followed back to Dock Road. Just before the Lifeboat Station, turn left and climb steps onto a path, the line of an old railway, which runs above the coast. Once through a strip of woodland the path descends to Mount Road. Turn right then left onto Tower Road, proceed through Well Square and follow Church Road to the right back to Dock Road. Turn left, return to Berwick Bridge, cross the Tweed onto Bridge End and follow West Street back to Marygate.

archway and climb onto the Town Walls. Ahead is The Lions, a large villa, which Lowry considered buying in 1947 but was put off by its then poor condition. Turn right, walk past Berwick Barracks and a football pitch which Lowry incorporated into his picture *Going to the Match*, which sold for £1.9 million in 1999.

At a crossroads go left and follow the path over Scots Gate, enjoying Lowry's favourite view of the Town Hall. Beyond a gate, descend to Bankhill, keeping right where it forks and pass underneath

Berwick to Queensferry Coastal Trail

Cliff scenery, St Abb's Head

7 he 145km (90 miles) between Berwick-upon-Tweed and Queensferry provide everything a long distance path should have – exceptional scenery, interesting locations, outstanding wildlife and a good selection of accommodation, shops, cafes and restaurants.

This chapter describes the route as a 7-day walk. However, the close proximity of towns and villages with regular buses, linking in with the main East Coast train line between Edinburgh and Berwick-upon-Tweed, means the route can be started or finished almost anywhere.

However it is approached, this is a route of great beauty and interest along predominantly good paths and easily attainable for reasonably fit walkers.

Nevertheless, rougher terrain will be encountered at points with a few steep ascents and descents, and some sections may require map-reading skills, but in general the route is simple to follow and utterly absorbing.

Berwick-upon-Tweed is easily reached from Edinburgh and the route is described from south to north, for anyone interested in continuing the North Sea Trail round Scotland's East Coast via the existing Fife Coastal Path and the Angus and Aberdeenshire Coastal Paths, which are currently in development.

Day 1 runs from **Berwick-upon-Tweed to St Abbs** [54] following the excellent paths and waymarks of the Berwickshire Coastal Path across a diverse landscape, from cliff-tops, to beach and through villages and towns like Burnmouth and Eyemouth to arrive at St Abbs gorgeous little harbour.

Day 2 is perhaps the most spectacular. Certainly the initial stages of the route from **St Abbs to Cockburnspath** [55] travel across some of Britain's finest scenery, passing through St Abb's Nature Reserve and along an incredible cliff-top path (where the birdlife is staggering) that extends almost all the way to Dowlaw.

Quiet roads and paths then lead past the likes of Pease Bay and Cove Bay to reach the welcoming village of Cockburnspath.

Day 3 runs from **Cockburnspath to Dunbar** [56] and although only 16km (10 miles) in length and the shortest section of the route, some rough terrain has to be crossed and, consequently, it is a harder day than at first might be envisaged. However cliff-top paths present far-reaching views along the Scottish Borders and East Lothian coastlines and the final approach to Dunbar is thoroughly enjoyable.

Day 4 from **Dunbar to North Berwick** [57] follows the John Muir Way and at 24km (15 miles) is the longest section of the route. After taking in the wildlife rich John Muir Country Park, the walk heads inland to East Linton and then through attractive countryside into the warm and welcoming coastal town of North Berwick.

On **Day 5** the landscape begins to soften, with cliffs and rugged headlands being replaced by expansive sandy beaches, and almost all of the 23km (14.25 miles) from **North Berwick to Cockenzie** [58] is along the coast. Like the previous day, the route follows the well waymarked paths of the John Muir Way, with Edinburgh and the Pentland Hills conspicuous on the horizon.

Day 6 from **Cockenzie to Leith** [59]

sticks predominantly to the coast. The John Muir Way ends at Fisherrow, but the route continues along the coastline of the Firth of Forth. The walking is generally simple with no real navigational issues and the terrain through Joppa and Portobello remains fairly flat, all the way to the lively Edinburgh suburb of Leith; a great spot to relax and enjoy the hospitality.

Day 7, the final stage from **Leith to Queensferry** [60], journeys through a primarily urban environment, but it hugs the coast for most of its 20km (12.75 miles) and remains a joy to walk. Once away from Leith, the seaside terraces and esplanades of Newhaven give way to industry and urban renewal at Grantown. However, it isn't long before the coast is gained again and the open grassy spaces of Silverknowes lead to the historic village of Cramond. From here the River Almond Walkway is followed a short distance inland, before returning to the coast through the woodlands of Dalmeny Estate.

The final section along the Firth of Forth Coast offers pleasant woodland walking on paths and estate roads to reach historic Queensferry and its iconic rail and road bridge.

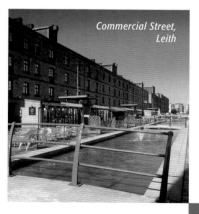

Commercial Street, Leith

SERVICES

A wide range of accommmmodation is available along the coast. Advance booking is recommended. Other locations can be found at <www.visitscotland.com>.

Wild camping is allowed on the coast if exercised in accordance with the Land Reform (Scotland) Act 2003 and the Scottish Access Code <www.outdooraccess-scotland.com>. Please avoid open fires, bury human waste and take your rubbish home.

BERWICK-UPON-TWEED

Accommodation
Travelodge North Road, TD15 1UQ;
(0871 984 6279)
The Queens Head, 6 Sandgate, TD15 1EP;
(01289 307852)
The Castle, 103 Castlegate, TD15 1LF;
(01289 307900)
The Kings Arms, 43 Hide Hill, TD15 1EJ;
(01289 307454)

Facilities
Pubs, shops and restaurants, post office, rail station. Visitor Information Centre, 106 Marygate, TD15 1BN; (01670 622155)

EYEMOUTH

Accommodation
Eye Sleep Over, Toll Bridge Road, TD14 5GN; (01890 750913)
Hillcrest B+B, Coldingham Rd, TD14 5AN; (01890 752993)
Ship Hotel, Harbour Rd, TD14 5HT; (01890 750224)
The Dolphin Hotel, North Street, TD14 5ES; (01890 750280)

Facilities
Pubs, shops and restaurants, post office. Visitor Information Centre, Market Place, TD14 5HE; (01890 750678)

COLDINGHAM

Accommodation
Courtburn House, School Rd, TD14 5NS; (01890 750280)
St Vedas Hotel, Coldingham Bay, TD14 5PA; (01890 771679)
Priory View, Eyemouth Road, TD14 5NH; (01890 771525)
Rhovanion B+B, St Abbs Road, TD14 5NR; (01890 771760)

Facilities
Pubs, shops and restaurants, post office. Visitor Information Centre, Bridge Street, TD14 5NS; (01890 771492)

ST ABBS

Facilities
Pubs, shops and restaurants, post office.

DUNBAR

Accommodation
Bayswell, 16 Bayswell Park, EH42 1AE; (01368 862225)
The Rocks, Marine Rd, EH42 1DD; (01368 862287)
Royal McIntosh Hotel, Station Rd, EH42 1JY; (01368 238002)
Castle Hotel, 163 High Street, EH42 1ES; (01368 862711)
Springfield B+B, Belhaven Road, EH42 1NH; (01368 862502)
Belhaven Bay Campsite, Edinburgh Road, EH42 1TU; (01368 865956)

Facilities
Pubs, shops and restaurants, post office, rail station. Visitor Information Centre, 143 High Street, EH42 1ES; (01368 863353)

EAST LINTON

Accommodation
The Linton Hotel, 3 Bridgend, EH40 3AF; (01620 860202)

Facilities
Pubs, shops and restaurants, post office.

NORTH BERWICK

Accommodation
County Hotel, 15-17 High Street, EH39 4HH; (01620 892989)
Nether Abbey Hotel, 20 Dirleton Avenue, EH39 4BQ; (01620 892802)
Blenheim House Hotel, 14 Westgate, EH39 4AF; (01620 892385)
Seaholm B+B, 24 Melbourne Rd, EH39 4LB; (01620 895150)
Kaimend B+B, Hamilton Rd, EH39 4NA; (01620 893557)
Tantallon Caravan & Camping Park, Dunbar Road, EH39 5NJ; (01620 893348)

Facilities
Pubs, shops and restaurants, post office. rail station. Visitor Information Centre, Quality Street EH39 4HJ; (01620 892197)

DIRLETON

Accommodation
The Castle Inn, Manse Road, EH39, 5EP; (01620 850221)

GULLANE

Accommodation

Greywalls, Duncur Rd, EH31 2EG;
(01620 842144)
The Golf Inn, Main St, EH31 2AB;
(01620 843259)
Bissetts, Main St, EH31 2AA;
(01620 843146)
Kilmory B+B, Marine Terrace, EH31 2AZ;
(01620 842332)
Jadini Garden B&B, Goose Green, EH31
2BA; (01620 843343)

Facilities

Pubs, shops and restaurants, post office.

ABERLADY

Accommodation

The Old Aberlady Inn, West Main St, EH32
0RF; (01875 870503)
West Craig, 32 High St, EH32 0RA;
(07905 975548)

Facilities

Pubs, shops and restaurants, post office.

LONGNIDDRY

Accommodation

St. Germains B+B, 2 St. Germains House,
EH32 0PQ; (01875 853034)
Seton Sands Holiday Park, Seton Sands,
EH32 0QF; (01875 813 333)

Facilities

Pubs, shops and restaurants, post office, rail
station.

COCKENZIE & PORT SEATON

Accommodation

Anchorage B+B, 1 Elcho Place, EH32 0DL;
(01875 813947)

Facilities

Pubs, shops and restaurants, post office.

PRESTONPANS

Facilities

Pubs, shops and restaurants, post office, rail
station.

MUSSELBURGH

Accommodation

Premier Inn Carberry Rd, EH21 8PT;
(0871 527 8358)
Eildon B+B, 109 Newbigging, EH21 7AS;
(0131 665 3981)
Ravelston House, 182 North High Street,

EH21 6BH; (0131 665 2478)
Creag House, Carberry Road, EH21 8PT;
(0131 665 3005)
Drum Mohr Campsite, Levenhall, EH21 8JS;
(01316 656867)

Facilities

Pubs, shops and restaurants, post office.

PORTOBELLO & JOPPA

Accommodation

Seahaven Hotel, 89 Joppa Rd, EH15 2HB;
(0131 669 4592)
Abercorn Guest House, 1 Abercorn Terrace,
EH15 2DD; (0131 669 6139)
Rockville Hotel, 2 Joppa Rd, EH15 2HF;
(0131 669 5418)
Seabreeze B+B, 1 Seaview Terrace, EH15
2HD; (0131 657 3842)

Facilities

Pubs, shops and restaurants, post office.

PORT OF LEITH

Accommodation

Holiday Inn Express, The Royal Yacht
Britannia, EH6 6JJ; (0871 902 1610)
Malmaison, 1 Tower Place, EH6 7BZ;
(0844 693 0652)
Parkview House Hotel, 14 Hermitage Place,
EH6 8AF; (0131 554 6206)

Facilities

Pubs, shops and restaurants, post office.

CRAMOND

Facilities

Pubs, shops and restaurants, post office.

QUEENSFERRY

Accommodation

Orocco Pier Hotel, 17 High St, EH30 9PP;
(0870 118 1664)
The Hawes Inn, 7 Newhalls Rd, EH30 9TA;
(0131 331 1990)
Staghead Hotel, 8 High St, EH30 9PP;
(0131 331 1039)
Priory Lodge, 8 The Loan, EH30 9NS;
(0131 331 4345)

Facilities

Pubs, shops and restaurants, post office, rail
station..

PUBLIC TRANSPORT

The Edinburgh, East Lothian and Scottish
Borders coast is well served by public trans-
port. For train and bus contact details see
Using this Guidebook on page 11..

Lamberton Skerrs

The coastal trail begins its long journey at Berwick-upon-Tweed and strikes its course north-west for 22.5km to the little village of St Abbs. Good paths line the route, which travels along a jagged, picturesque coastline, passing through Burnmouth and Eyemouth en route.

From the Town Hall on Marygate walk along Woolmarket to Ravensdowne. Climb some steps onto the Town Walls then follow a narrow lane past the impressive Lions House. At a junction go right then left down a flight of steps and under an archway. At a fork keep right and follow the path away from the Town Walls. After a row of houses a path crosses the edge of Berwick Cricket Club. Once through a car park turn left to gain the Berwickshire Coastal Path.

A path runs to the right of Magdalene Fields Golf Course, with great views along the coastline. Once past a coast-guard watchtower turn right onto a tarmac golf course path, then near the clubhouse and just before a car park, turn right and follow a path right of a caravan park and above Fisherman's Haven. The path hugs the coastline, eventually swinging left to reach a three-way junction.

Go right, signposted for Marshall Meadows, and continue north-west high above the coast, strewn with caves and sea-stacks. A broad path soon runs in-between a railway line and the coast to Marshall Meadows caravan site. Cross a stile, turn right and follow a road through the caravan site, bearing left at a fork then right at a junction. A fenced grassy track runs above Marshall Meadows Bay to the border between England and Scotland.

Go through a gate, turn left and walk along a field edge path to a wall. Turn right into Scotland, where the path follows coastal and field-edge paths,

START : Town Hall, Berwick-upon-Tweed (NT999529)
DISTANCE: 22.5km; 14 miles
TIME: 7hrs

MAP: OS 67 & 75
TERRAIN: Roads, coastal paths & beach
GRADE: Moderate/Strenuous

Burnmouth harbour

Berwick-upon-Tweed

passing the lonely ruin at Lamberton Skerrs and through a few gates to Lamberton Holdings. Follow a path to the left of a narrow road and after 100m turn right down steps then left onto the road, which climbs steadily through open countryside. Before the road turns left to pass under the railway line, turn right over a waymarked stile and descend a field-edge path to a waymarked gate. Turn left over a stile where a path zigzags down a steep hillside to the shore of Burnmouth Bay.

Turn left, follow the main road through the quiet village, passing Burnmouth harbour and the poignant memorial to the Eyemouth Disaster. The road climbs steeply to Burnmouth Kirk, where a path runs to the right of the church and ascends steps to a narrow road. Turn left, then climb steeply to a junction. Turn right, then right again after a primary school onto a road, turn left at a path signposted Eyemouth and follow it right onto a field-edge path on Burnmouth Hill.

This undulates gently north along the scenic coastline, which holds remarkable geological formations. Eventually a waymark is reached, pointing right and straight on. Keep straight on then begin to descend gradually alongside Eyemouth golf course. Bear left at the

next waymark and then, upon reaching a sign for Eyemouth, turn left through a gate, where a path crosses the golf course to a road. Turn right and descend the pavement to Eyemouth Harbour.

Turn left, follow the quayside by Gunsgreen House and cross a bridge over the Eye Water. At the end of the harbour turn right over the river again then right onto Harbour Road. At Marine Parade turn left, walk through Eyemouth then go right onto a beach just before the leisure centre. Follow the beach to steps on the left, which climb high above the coast and pass a few caravans to a fork. Go left along the cliffs of Killiedraught Bay, relishing superb views to St Abbs.

In time the path turns right down steps and crosses two footbridges onto Linkim Shore. Cross the beach, climb a steep path, which subsequently drops down by Yellow Craig Head and across a bridge over Milldown Burn. After another steep climb the path sweeps left down onto gorgeous Coldingham Bay. Walk across the sand, climb onto a paved path, turn right and walk into St Abbs.

At a fork go left onto Murrayfield, pass the post office then turn right onto Seaview Terrace. Walk down a path to St Abbs Harbour.

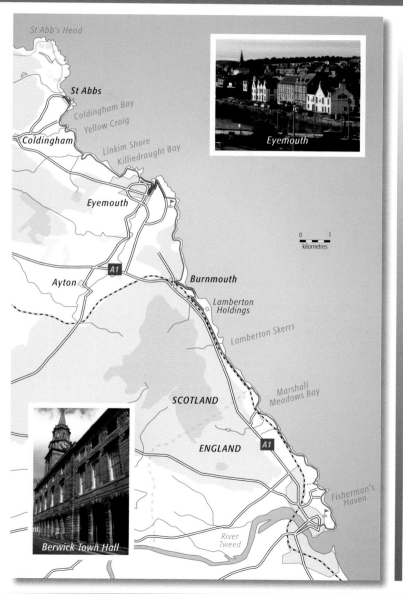

St Abb's Head

St Abbs

Coldingham Bay

Yellow Craig

Coldingham

Linkim Shore

Killiedraught Bay

Eyemouth

Eyemouth

0   1
kilometres

A1

Ayton

Burnmouth

Lamberton Holdings

Lamberton Skerrs

Marshall Meadows Bay

SCOTLAND

ENGLAND

A1

Fisherman's Haven

Berwick Town Hall

River Tweed

55 St Abbs to Cockburnspath

Day 2 – Berwickshire Coastal Path & Southern Upland Way

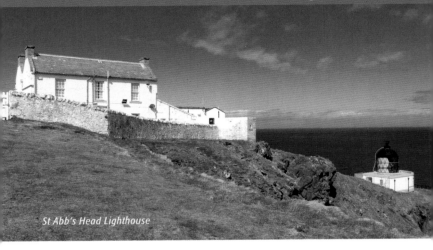

St Abb's Head Lighthouse

Spectacular cliff-top paths, field edges and quiet roads are all utlised on this stunning 22.5km stretch. There are several steep ascents, particularly in the first half of the route.

From St Abbs Harbour climb steps in-between two houses at the corner of the car park. At the top ascend the main road out of the village for 100m to a footpath on the left, which runs parallel to the road. At its end cross the main road onto another path signposted St Abb's Head and follow this through a gate to begin a steady ascent along cliffs towards the coast. In due course descend quite steeply past Horsecastle Bay.

After a gate, continue to climb in-between two embankments and bear left onto another path. Climb to reach St Abbs Head Lighthouse and some stunning views along the coast.

Keep to the left of the lighthouse buildings then descend the narrow access road to Pettico Wick. Once over a cattle grid turn right through a pedestrian gate signposted for Westerside Dean. Walk along the right edge of a field, climbing steadily to a stile. Once across turn right, cross another stile, then go left and ascend steeply onto the cliff-tops. With a fence to the left follow a cliff path, with precipitous drops to the right, pass through a gate and an Admiralty Mile Marker, the first of two sets of poles across a measured mile, used by shipping companies to test the speed of ocean going vessels.

In due course descend to cross a stile on the left. Keep right through gorse then turn right over two stiles. Walk along field edges (where livestock may graze) climbing over the prehistoric Tun Law forts, the highest points on the line of the Berwickshire coast.

The path soon swings left and drops down through a gate. Turn right through a gap in a wall then descend

START : St Abbs Harbour
(NT920673)

MAP: OS 67

DISTANCE: 22.5km; 14 miles

TERRAIN: Roads & coastal paths

TIME: 7hrs

GRADE: Strenuous

steeply alongside the wall. Beyond a gate walk right, descend across a footbridge over the Moor Burn at Westerside Dean. At the cliff edge, the burn forms a waterfall which plunges 30 metres to the shore below.

Another steep climb leads back onto the cliff-tops. After a gate the gradient eases as the route travels along field edges and past the second Admiralty Mile Marker. Keep on through a number of gates then turn right onto a grassy track. This sweeps left past a gate to reach the Old Post Road. Turn right for Dowlaw, follow a track, again bearing left just before a gate from where it descends over a field then a stone bridge across the Dowlaw Burn.

After a gate, follow the right edge of a field for 100m and bear right over a

stile. A steady climb to the right of a wall reaches a gate just before Dowlaw Farm. Go through here, turn right and follow waymarks through two gates. Cross a track into woodland and walk past the farm, exiting left onto a single-track access road.

Follow this across Coldingham Moor for just over 1km, crossing a cattle grid en route. Just before a second cattle grid bear right onto a rough waymarked path, which keeps to the left of a wall then turns right through a gate opposite a communications aerial and the disused Dowlaw Quarry.

A fenced path descends towards the coast. Pass through a gate then walk along field edges through a number of gates to a waymarked gate on the right. Again follow the waymarks

Cliifs west of Pettico Wick

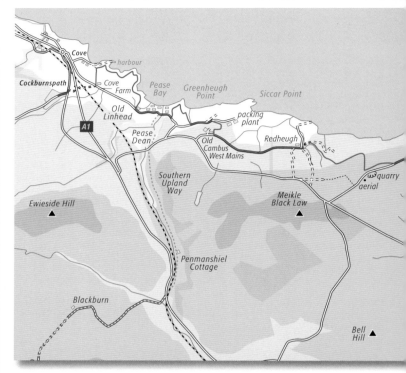

through several gates, eventually
turning left onto a farm track and
follow it through Redheugh Farm
to a minor road.

Follow the road past Old Cambus East
Mains and ascend for 600m towards
the row of cottages at Old Cambus
West Mains. Just before the first, turn
right onto a field path signposted for
Pease Bay. This swings right then left
through a gate and drops down onto
another minor road. Turn left, walk past
Siccar Point car park, and after 300m
go right, just after a cattle grid, through
a gate for Pease Bay.

A wonderful coastal path rounds
Greenheugh Point then descends steps
to a narrow road. Walk right, cross a
footbridge over a ford and pass Pease
Bay Leisure Park. Climb the road and at
Old Linhead turn right through a gate
to join the Southern Upland Way which
crosses a footbridge and continues
round the coast past Cove Harbour.

Just before Cove turn left through a
gate for Cockburnspath where a path
heads inland. At a crossroads go
straight on then, at a junction, turn left
then right. A track passes some
cottages then goes under a railway
line. Keep right, pass beneath the A1
and continue into Cockburnspath. Turn
left then right onto Hoprig Road to
finish at The Square.

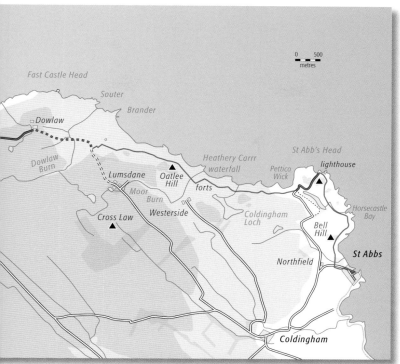

0 500
metres

Fast Castle Head

Souter

Brander

Dowlaw

Dowlaw
Burn

Lumsdane

Moor
Burn

Westerside

Cross Law

Oatlee
Hill

Heathery Carrr
waterfall

forts

Coldingham
Loch

Northfield

St Abb's Head

Pettico
Wick

lighthouse

Horsecastle
Bay

Bell
Hill

St Abbs

Coldingham

Cove harbour & Torness

Above Thorntonloch

*A*lthough the 16km from Cockburnspath to Dunbar is the shortest section of the coastal path, it is actually one of the toughest, with some rough terrain underfoot and stony beaches to cross. However the route also travels over quiet beaches, around secluded bays and along cliff-tops, hugging the coastline for the majority of the day with spectacular views throughout.

From Cockburnspath walk north through the village, following the road as it bears left to a roundabout at the A1. Turn left onto a quiet road, pass underneath a railway bridge then cross a bridge over the Dunglass Burn to a track on the right opposite East Lodge. Follow the track under a railway arch then immediately turn right onto the John Muir Way. A path descends through woodland, passing underneath two bridges. At a road go straight across through a gate and descend above the Dunglass Burn through woodland onto a stony beach.

Turn left, cross the beach, where loose stones can be awkward underfoot, for approximately 300m to a waymark. Bear left onto a path, cross a bridge then swing left to climb through woodland to a spectacular waterfall. Turn right up steps and follow a path out of woodland onto a superb field edge path, which heads north-west high above the coast. The view of the East Lothian and Scottish Borders coastline is spectacular.

The path runs to the left of a wall then a fence, with steep slopes dropping right to the shore below. In due course it swings left around a gorge and goes through a gate to continue high along the coast, with fine views of

START : Cockburnspath (NT776711)

DISTANCE: 16km; 10 miles

TIME: 6hrs

MAP: OS 67

TERRAIN: Roads, tracks, coastal paths & beach

GRADE: Moderate/Strenuous

Thortonloch and Torness ahead. The path eventually veers left through a gate and descends to a footbridge. Cross the bridge, follow a narrow path along a gorgeous beach and by a cottage, then turn left to cross the Thorton Burn via a bridge. Turn right, drop down onto the beach and walk past a caravan site (if high tide makes the beach impassable, then walkers are allowed to walk through the site).

Once by the site, turn left from the beach, follow a path through a gate and past the caravan site to a road on the right. Walk towards Torness then go right at a junction from where a man-made walkway leads around the coastal side of Torness Power Station.

Once off the walkway climb steps onto a path high above Skateraw Bay, then drop down through a car park and onto a road. At a cottage go right, walk along a rough track beside Skateraw Bay and go around a gate where a path reaches a beach at Chapel Point. Turn left, follow a path, dropping briefly onto the stony beach, then continue as the path swings left to cross a bridge over the Dry Burn. Bear right where a fine coastal path continues easily for 1.75km to Barns Ness Lighthouse.

Turn left walk along an access road then turn right around a gate onto a stony track. Follow this by an old limekiln then drop down through a gate to a car park at Catcraig. Walk along an access road and just before its entrance turn right then left onto a rough path, which goes around the beautiful White Sands. The path quickly improves as it gains Dunbar Golf Course. Keep to its coastal edge (keeping an eye out for golfers and golf balls) following a combination of paths and tracks along

the wonderfully rugged coastline.

Once by a stone shelter the golf course narrows and there are tremendous views of Dunbar ahead. A bridge crosses the Spott Burn to gain a gravel path, which in turn crosses a stone bridge. As the track swings left, bear right onto a grassy path, which passes Dunbar Golf Course clubhouse onto a promenade.

Just before East Beach, on the outskirts of Dunbar, turn left onto Golf House Road then right onto East Links Road and follow it into Dunbar, turning right onto Woodbush Brae then left onto Woodbush. Follow this onto Lamer Street, then cross Victoria Street onto Victoria Place at Victoria Harbour. From here, Castle Gate can be followed uphill to Victoria Street and Dunbar High Street.

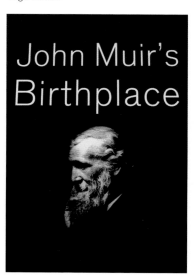

John Muir's Birthplace

Dunbar

East Beach

Broxmouth

White Sands

quarry

Catcraig

Spott Burn

A1

cement works

quarry

Doon Hill

A1

Brunt Hill

Innerwick

Cocklaw Hill

Dunglass Burn

0   500
metres

Day 3 - Cockburnspath to Dunbar

Dunbar from the east

Barns Ness

Chapel Point

Dry Burn

Skateraw

Skateraw Bay

Torness Point

Torness Power Station

Thorntonloch

Thornton Burn

A1

Bilsdean Creek

Bilsdean

Dunglass

Cove

Dunglass Burn

Cockburnspath

A1

57 Dunbar to North Berwick
Day 4 – John Muir Way

Hedderwick Hill Plantation

tage 4 of the coastal trail is bookended by Dunbar and North Berwick and heads inland where East Lothian's rural environs are equally alluring as its coast. Consequently these 24km may well be the finest of the entire route. A lovely section of the River Tyne (where kingfisher are regularly spotted) leads into lovely East Linton, home to the historic Preston Mill and a good place for a break.

From the north end of Dunbar High Street, bear left onto Bayswell Road then turn right through a pair of stone pillars. Walk down steps then follow a paved path above the coast. Descend then ascend some steps, turn left up more steps, pass through a stone archway, ascend another flight of steps then turn right onto a cliff-top esplanade, which grants beautiful views west towards Belhaven Bay.

When the esplanade ends turn left down two flights of steps and follow a path around the edge of Winterfield Golf Course to reach Shore Road on the edge of Belhaven Bay. Follow the road round and past a car park to a path on the right, signposted John Muir Way. Follow the path and wall along the southern edge of Belhaven Bay to meet the Biel Water.

Go over the footbridge, turn right, and continue north-west through coastal grassland into the heart of John Muir Country Park. At a fork go left then right before a car park. At the next fork turn left onto a narrower path, which follows the southern edge of Hedderwick Hill Plantation to Hedderwick Sands and a footbridge over the Hedderwick Burn.

Cross over and continue on a path running above the shore beside concrete anti-tank blocks, to gain a

START : Dunbar High Street
(NT679790)

MAP: OS 66 & 67

DISTANCE: 24km; 15 miles

TERRAIN: Roads, tracks & paths

TIME: 7hrs

GRADE: Moderate/Strenuous

rough access road just north of Tynefield. Turn right and follow the road as it swings left through beautiful countryside, passing the entrance to Kirklandhill Farm. Just before the A198 turn right, follow a field-edge path into woodland beside the River Tyne. Turn left under a road bridge then walk south-west along a fabulous section of the River Tyne to a weir.

Turn right, cross a footbridge spanning the Tyne, then over a stone bridge onto a minor road. At a fork go left, follow the road onto a field-edge path, to the right of the Tyne, which is crossed again at a bridge near to the curiously named Phantassie. Turn right, follow another field-edge path, crossing the Tyne for a third time to a fork. Go left (the right fork leads to Preston Mill) and beyond a gate and another bridge turn left onto Preston Road (B1407) and continue into East Linton.

At High Street go right, and walk out of the village. Opposite Dunpender Road turn right through a gate, climb a path through a gap in a wall, turn left and climb some steps onto a track

which ascends over Drylaw Hill, granting expansive views towards North Berwick Law.

The track drops gradually from Drylaw and heads north through fine countryside. At a junction go straight on where a path is easily followed through fields to a left turn across two bridges. Once by a pocket of woodland the path passes to the right of Kamehill to a road. Cross this onto a track then at the next junction turn left then right and follow a minor road by Stonelaws and Old Stonelaws. At the next junction go straight across through a gate, turn left and follow a field-edge path into Craigmoor Wood.

Continue around the right edge of the wood, eventually dropping down to a road. Turn right then immediately left through East Wood, exiting into a field. Turn right, follow a path as it swings left, then left again to cross another field. Just before a gate turn right, and continue along the path, passing through a gate onto a minor road near Wamphrey.

Follow this left to a waymarked gate on the right. Beyond this a field-edge path heads north, crossing a road then climbing gently to bear right through a gate. A path drops down by North Berwick Law and through a car park onto Wishart Terrace. Turn right onto Lochbridge Road and at a waymark, turn left over Gilbert Avenue. Walk through a pocket of woodland and across Couper Avenue, then continue down Lady Jane Avenue. Cross St Baldred's Road into the grounds of North Berwick Lodge. Go over a path, then turn left at a fork and descend through the park onto Kirk Ports Road, continuing straight ahead to finish on Quality Street.

Red Campion

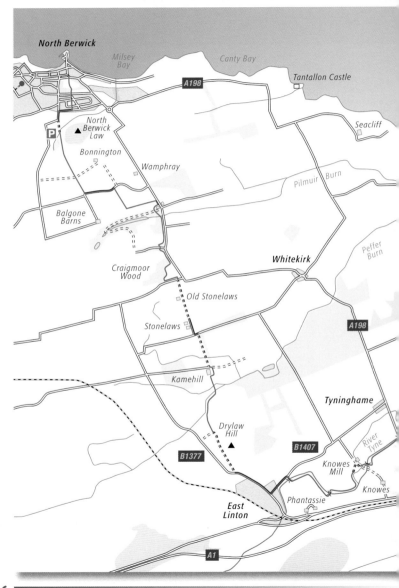

North Berwick Law
from Drylaw Hill

Peffer Sands

Ravensheugh Sands

St Baldred's Cradle

0 ___ 500
metres

Sandy
Hirst

Belhaven
Bay

Hedderwick Hill

Dunbar

klandhill Tynefield

West
Barns

A1

A1

Biel Water

Fidra & the
Fife Coast from
Yellowcraig

The 23km between North Berwick and Cockenzie are almost entirely along the East Lothian coastline. The route only heads inland from Yellowcraig to pass through the delightful surrounds of Dirleton and Gullane, before heading back to the coast at Aberlady Bay. From there it's glorious coastal walking all the way to Cockenzie.

From Quality Street turn left onto High Street, right onto Church Road then left along Beach Road. Bear right around the front of the North Berwick Clubhouse to Pointgarry Road. Turn right, walk past a car park and left onto Links Road, which climbs to York Road. Turn right here then right again at Upper Kaimend.

Go left at a waymark, then beyond a gate turn left again, following the edge of a golf course and once through another gate turn right where a path culminates at Strathern Road. Turn right onto Abbotsford Road, follow this to its end, then take a path on the right. Go through a gate and turn left along another path, which in turn travels around the perimeter wall of Invereil House.

Once through a gate turn right at a waymark where a path heads diagonally across a field. Beyond two more gates, walk through coastal grassland to a fork. Turn left, then at a crossroads go left and follow the path to a junction where a left turn heads towards Yellowcraig. Just before the car park turn right onto a woodland path (signposted Dirleton). At the next waymark turn left then right to follow a field edge path and after approximately 50m bear left to head south along a track through fields to gain Manse

START : North Berwick Quality Street (NT555853)

DISTANCE: 23km; 14.25 miles

TIME: 7hrs

MAP: OS 66

TERRAIN: Roads, tracks & coastal paths

GRADE: Moderate/Strenuous

Road and Dirleton.

Just before the village green turn right through a gate and walk along a disused road beside Archerfield Links Golf Course. At a junction with the course access road, follow it left for 20m then cross over onto a waymarked track which leads through fields to woodland, exiting via a gate onto the pavement beside the A198. Turn right and follow this into Gullane.

At Saltcoats Road turn left, go straight on past Templar Place and follow a single-track road, turning right at waymark. At the next waymark bear right, pass through a gate and after 20m, beside a dismantled railway, go right at a fork. Pass through another gate and follow a path left of Luffness Links, to exit onto the A198 beyond Luffness Links Clubhouse.

Carefully cross the busy road, turn left and follow the pavement round Aberlady Bay and through Aberlady past Aberlady Parish Church. Leave the pavement at a waymark onto a woodland path on the right. Once across the entrance drive to Green Craigs Hotel, follow the path through more woodland, exiting over a footbridge and going left at a fork to walk above Gosford Bay. In due course bear left into a strip of woodland, the path running alongside the A198. Leave the woodland onto a broad track, which immediately forks. The left fork heads through Longniddry Bents Gosford Car Park at Ferny Ness.

Keep straight ahead at a fork from where the road soon swings left then right by the car park entrance. Once away from the car park a path continues through dune grass to a fork opposite the Longniddry Road. Go right

and cross a burn over a footbridge onto a sandy path. At a fork keep right and walk around a rockier headland. Once over another footbridge go straight on through a strip of woodland then through Longniddry Bents Car Park No2.

The path then forks left, leading through woodland and along dunes, eventually dropping down through Longniddry Bents Car Park No1. A sandy path descends through another car park then crosses a footbridge over a burn. Keep on towards Seton Sands but just before Seton Sands Caravan Park turn left at a waymark to the B1348. Turn right and follow the pavement above Seton Sands.

Just after entering Cockenzie and Port Seton turn right at a waymark onto a promenade. Follow this by Wrecked Craigs to Port Seton Harbour. Bear left around the harbour, pass through a gap in a fence and bear right onto Viewforth. Follow Wemyss Place by the harbour then turn right onto a paved path, which runs above the shore, passing through a small car park and down some steps to Cockenzie Harbour.

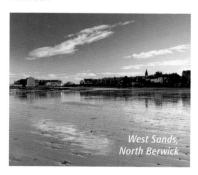

West Sands, North Berwick

Cockenzie & Edinburgh from Longniddry Bents

Gull
Lin

Gullane Sands

Aberlady Bay

Craigielaw Point

Aberlady

Gosford Sands

Gosford
House

0   500
metres

Cockenzie &
Port Seton

Seton Sands

Longniddry

power
station

holiday
homes

A198

Fidra

Broad Sands

North Berwick

Milsey Bay

Archerfield

Yellow-craig

A198

North Berwick Law

'ane 'y

Gullane

A198

Dirlton

Saltcoats

Craigmoor Wood

Near Dirlton

Haddington A1

Cockenzie to Leith
Day 6 – John Muir Way & Firth of Forth Coast

Leith Docks

*L*ike the previous stage, the walk between Cockenzie to Leith sticks predominantly to the coastline but travels through a much more urban environment. Prestonpans, Musselburgh, Fisherrow (where the John Muir Way ends) and Portobello are all interesting and attractive suburbs of Edinburgh and the famed skyline of Scotland's capital city is a constant image throughout this stage, which concludes at the lively and historic setting of the Port of Leith.

From Cockenzie Harbour turn left and follow West Harbour Road to Edinburgh Road. Turn right then bear right and follow a path across a park beside Cockenzie Power Station. Cross a bridge onto a promenade, which swings left to travel south-west along the coast by the power station and a

pier. Once through a gate follow a path over grassland towards Prestonpans.

Upon reaching a junction go right then left at a fork to Edinburgh road. Turn right into Prestonpans, walk along High Street then turn right at a waymark. The path now swings left along the coast. Once up a flight of steps turn right and follow the path back to High Street, then turn right and leave Prestonpans.

Just after Inchview North turn right at a waymark and follow a path back to the coast. It then swings left and keeps on through the peaceful parkland of Morrison's Haven with amazing views of Edinburgh – keep an eye out for long-tailed duck, terns, kestrel and scoter.

Once by an information board bear left onto a path and follow this back to

START : *Cockenzie Harbour* (NT398757)

DISTANCE: *17km; 10.5 miles*

TIME: *5hrs 45mins*

MAP: *OS 66*

TERRAIN: *Roads, tracks & paths*

GRADE: *Moderate/Strenuous*

the B1348. Turn right, walk along the pavement by the entrance to Prestongrange Museum and then after approx 100m turn right then left into Levenhall Links. Beyond a gate turn right where a path returns to the shore and bears left to run alongside a seawall, eventually sweeping left at the mouth of the River Esk.

Bear right onto a grassy path and go around a barrier onto Goose Green Place. Keep straight on along Goosegreen Crescent then turn right and cross the River Esk via a footbridge. Turn right onto a riverbank path, which swings left onto open parkland. Go straight across Mountjoy Terrace then right where a path crosses more grass-land into Fisherrow. The path goes right then immediately left onto Promenade to reach Fisherrow Harbour where the John Muir Way ends.

However, the coastal trail doesn't stop here. From Fisherrow Harbour, walk along New Street then bear right onto Edinburgh Road (A199) and follow the pavement out of Musselburgh onto Musselburgh Road (A199) and through Joppa. Continue by Rock Cottage and Joppa Pans to reach Portobello Beach. Either drop down onto the beach or take to Promenade (both provide great views of the Ochil Hills) through Portobello (there are various side streets that can be taken into Portobello).

Follow Promenade onto Promenade Terrace, pass around a barrier onto King's Place and go past a small car park. After another barrier a wide cycle-walkway, travels above the shore in-between some factories and a seawall, eventually reaching Seafield Road.

Bear right here, follow the pavement and just before a bridge crossing a railway line, bear right and descend a path, which then runs alongside the

Prestonpans mural

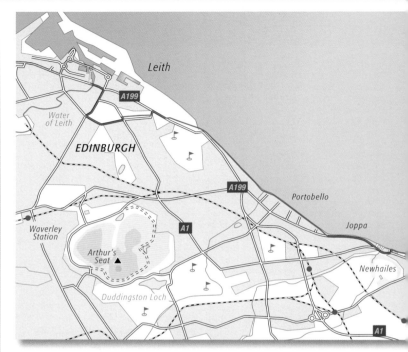

Portobello Swimming Pool

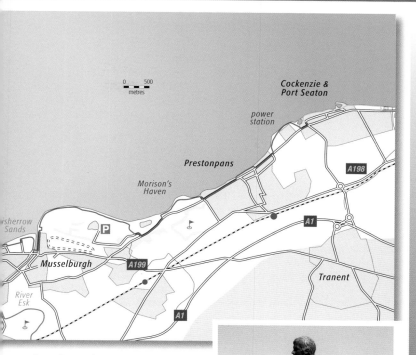

railway line and a fence to reach a single-track road. Turn left, cross a level crossing over the railway line then right, back onto Seafield Road.

At Seafield Place turn left where the route heads a little inland. At Leith Links turn right and follow a path diagonally through the park. Cross Links Gardens, turn left then right and continue in-between East Hermitage Place and Leith Links. At a junction bear right onto Duke Street, go past the old Leith Academy School and turn right onto Constitution Street and on to Bernard Street.

Turn left at the statue of Robert Burns and follow Bernard Street over the Water of Leith to finish on Commercial Street.

Robert Burns

Day 7 – Firth of Forth Coast & River Almond Walkway

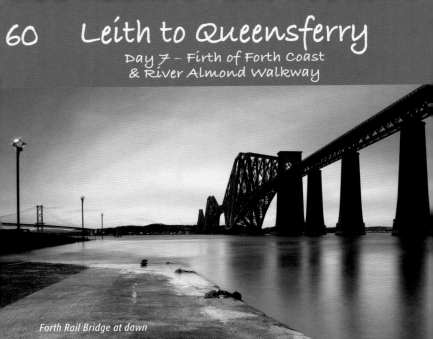

Forth Rail Bridge at dawn

2ueensferry marks the culmination of the 145km trail along the Berwickshire and Lothian coast and offers a selection of excellent pubs and restaurants in which to refuel and rest tired feet and legs.

The final 20km from the Port of Leith to Queensferry predominantly follows the coast, passing lovely Newhaven Harbour and Granton to reach Cramond. From there, the River Almond Walkway leads into Dalmeny Estates, and a wonderful final section through coastal woodlandt.

From the Water of Leith on Commercial Street, turn right onto Dock Street then left onto Commercial Quay. Turn right through a car park then go right alongside the Water of Leith by some flats to re-cross the Water of Leith by the Victoria Swing Bridge. Turn left and follow Ocean Drive, turning left by Ocean Terminal Shopping Centre then right onto Lindsay Road (A901).

Walk west to the attractive Newhaven Harbour where Charles Darwin studied geology and fossils when at Edinburgh University in 1825. Several very important fish fossils have been found at Newhaven, some more than 400 million years old.

From Newhaven follow the A901 above the Firth of Forth passing Granton Harbour. Continue by Granton Square onto West Harbour Road and pass the distinctive lighthouse which was built in 1845. In fact it never saw service as a lighthouse, but became a depot for shipping goods and equipment to offshore lighthouses along the coast.

Continue along West Shore Road, turn right onto a path signposted

START : *Leith Commercial Street (NT271766)*

FINISH: *Queensferry High Street (NT135783)*

DISTANCE: *20km; 12.5 miles*

TIME: *5hrs*

MAP: *OS 65 & 66*

TERRAIN: *Roads, tracks & paths*

GRADE: *Moderate/Strenuous*

Silverknowes and walk around Granton Point, turning right at a junction into Gypsy Brae Park. Follow the seafront promenade to Cramond Harbour from where there are superb views of Cramond Island and beyond to the Ochil Hills above Stirling.

Turn left onto Riverside and past Cramond Boat Club to the River Almond Walkway. A path proceeds through woodland, in due course passing by more houses and a car park onto another woodland path. Beyond an old stone building and an impressive weir, climb a flight of steps and continue above the river.

Another steep flight of steep steps ascend high above the River Almond then descend back down to the riverside path. At a fork go right, continue to Dowies Mill Lane, turn right and walk to Braepark Road.

Turn right, cross the River Almond by the impressive Cramond Brig (which is around 700 years old and in remarkable condition) onto Cramond Brig Toll.

Climb uphill and just before reaching the A90 turn right onto a track signposted for Queensferry. Follow this round a gate into Dalmeny Estates from where a fine track (Cycleway 76) leads through attractive countryside.

Once past East Craigie a narrow road continues for 750m. As the road swings left go straight on around a gate and descend a rough track into woodland. At a fork bear left and drop down to Eagle Rock where a path signposted 'Shore Walk' turns left.

Follow the shore walk past Snab Point and several secluded beaches to eventually reach a narrow road beside Long Green. Go straight across onto a woodland path. Beyond a footbridge the path runs alongside Dalmeny Estate Golf Course beside the broad swathe of Drum Sands. At a pocket of pine woodland it bears right to run above a beach, with the impressive Dalmeny House amidst parkland to the left.

As woodland is reached turn left onto an estate road then right into lovely

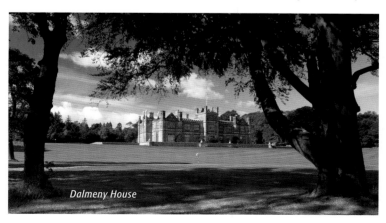

Dalmeny House

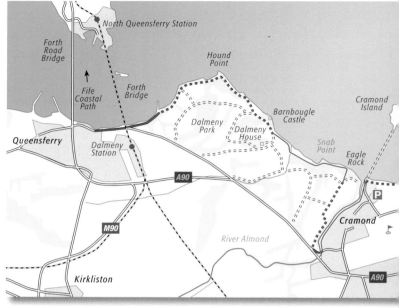

Leith Docks

broadleaved woodland to pass by Barnbougle Castle to a three-way junction. Take the centre path (Cycleway 76) and follow it along a gorgeous stretch of coastline passing some lovely quiet beaches.

In due course the path passes the secluded Fishery Cottage then rounds Hound Point towards Queensferry to eventually exit the woodland, with superb views of the Forth Road and Rail Bridges, onto a single-track road.

Pass by some cottages then Long Craig Pier to exit Dalmeny Estate as the road hugs the shoreline and passes underneath the Forth Rail Bridge onto Hawes Brae. Turn right and walk along the promenade, beside New Halls Road, enjoying superb views of the Firth of Forth to finish the coastal trail on High Street in the centre of Queensferry.

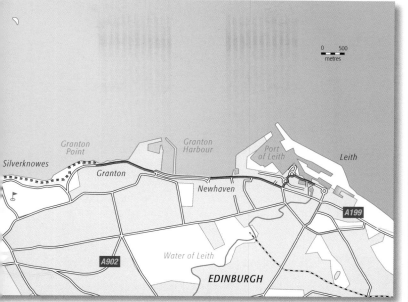

Silverknowes

Granton Point

Granton Harbour

Port of Leith

Leith

Granton

Newhaven

A199

A902

Water of Leith

EDINBURGH

0   500
metres

River Almond

mica *walkers' guides*
Available from high street and internet bookshops
www.micapublishing.com

Loch Lomond and The Trossachs National Park
Vol 1 – West *by Tom Prentice*

● 60 walks of 3 to 12 miles in and around Drymen, Aberfoyle, Callander, Strathyre, Lochearnhead and Killin

Loch Lomond and The Trossachs National Park
Vol 2 – East *by Tom Prentice*

● 60 walks of 3 to 12 miles in and around Luss, Arrochar, Lochgoilhead, Loch Eck, Crianlarich and Tyndrum

The Pentland Hills *by Rab Anderson*

● 60 walks of 3 to 12 miles in and around Colinton, Bonaly, Swanston, Hillend, Boghall, Flotterstone, Carlops, West Linton, Baddinsgill, Dunsire, Harlaw and Balerno

Scotland's Countryside Parks
Vol 1 – West *by Tom Prentice*

● 60 walks of 2 to 7 miles in Country Parks, Country Estates and Regional Parks

Scotland's Countryside Parks
Vol 2 – Edinburgh & East *by Tom Prentice*

● 60 walks of 2 to 7 miles in Country Parks, Country Estates and Regional Parks